THE
POST-GRADUATE

—AND—

Wooster Quarterly

NO. 68.—JULY, 1903.

A PLEA FOR HEDONISM.

JOHN C. PALMER, JR., PH. D., Wellsburg, W. Va.

A Graduating Thesis; Course A, Philosophy.

I. INTRODUCTORY.

It is the purpose of this essay to show that the ultimate ethical question is the question of the consequences of our actions. Ethics has to deal with human conduct and its consequences. The consequences of conduct determine the permissibility or advisability of the conduct. I expect further to show that it is the pleasant or painful consequences of our acts in which we are interested. If we were not sentient creatures, that is, if we merely had knowledge without any feeling of pleasure or pain in that knowledge, with that knowledge there would be no problem of conduct, for there would be no conduct. In other words, our sentience lies at the base of our activity.[1] To put the matter in terms of mechanics, it is because we find ourseves in unstable equilibrium, in a state of unrest or discomfort, that we act. Our actions are for the sake of establishing a new equilibrium in our sentient consciousness.

---

[1] See Taylor, The Problem of Conduct, Page 338.

In the following discussion, I assume that a man is a personality, a center of intelligent activity. He is different from the brook and the growing tree, even though we cannot state the difference in terms of human speech. He is different again from a mere creature of instinct and impulse. His intelligence makes him an original center of force, even though we cannot explain the nature of voluntary activity, or conduct. These assumptions are not intended to settle any metaphysical controversy. But unless we make such assumptions, man becomes a mere machine, an irresponsible and delusive mechanism. Ethics, from her place as the queen of science, is degraded to a subordinate place among the mechanical sciences. Such a conclusion would involve consequences too serious to be lightly accepted. If man is a machine, political science and theology are as meaningless as astrology and magic.[1]

Hedonism does not require the assumption of a purpose in the universe, yet it welcomes such an assumption, so long as one takes all the facts of human existence into account. Neither does Hedonism assume the immortality of the human soul, nor even its existence after death. But here again it welcomes any light which religion or theology can throw upon the subject of man's destiny. Starting with man as a sentient, intelligent consciousness, Hedonism seeks to determine his relation to the rest of Universe, and what share he has in the evolution of his destiny. We begin neither on the side of the Optimist nor the Pessimist, neither with the Stoic nor the Epicurean. With whom we shall end depends on evidence which shall be forthcoming.

As one reads treatise after treatise on the subject of ethics, he feels that the writers are, after all, consciously or unconsciously, striving to answer the same question and that question is: How may Human Welfare be Advanced? It does not matter that the real question is lost sight of in the midst of metaphysical and psychological meanderings. It is ever present, like the theme in a technical musical com-

---

[1] Cf. W. Wallace, Lectures and Essays, pages 250 and 251.

position. Metaphysical, psychological, and physiological discussions interest us, because we hope that they will throw some light on the ultimate question of human welfare and human destiny.

Ethics, is then, essentially a science of man, his welfare and his destiny. If ethics puts to itself the question, why should this thing be done, and that omitted, it is because the former tends to promote human welfare, while the latter would retard or prevent it.

But the term welfare is a broad, abstract term, about whose content and meaning there may be difference of opinion. Welfare is equivalent to doing or faring well. But what is "well"? The ethical problem, then, is merely stated when reduced to terms of human welfare. Before we can decide finally what is "well" for a man or for the human race, we should know something of the origin and nature of the individual and the race. We ought to know the place of man the individual, and man the species in the universe. From the standpoint of Hedonism, the problem of human conduct cannot receive a final solution till we are aware of every fact which can affect the consequences of human activity. But at the same time, the Hedonist insists on our making the best of such facts as are available. Because we are not aware of all the consequences of our acts, we are by no means justified in neglecting such consequences as are now familiar. Uncertainty as to the ultimate purpose or destiny of the race should not diminish my interest in my own personal destiny and welfare.

Prior to the nineteenth century, ignorance of man's nature and origin and his relation to the rest of the universe greatly hindered any intelligent answer to the question as to his place and function in the universe at large. So long as each individual was looked upon as a special piece of workmanship, shaped according to a set pattern, like a statue or a piano, it was impossible to arrive at a correct idea of man's place in Nature. But when the doctrine of evolution made it possible to study man as a growth, a mind among minds, an animal among animals and a living organism among living organisms, subject

to definite laws and principles, his present character and
future possibilities became a matter of supremest interest.
When we apply the doctrine of natural selection to man,
every trait of character and shade of temperament is
pregnant with meaning; every institution, past or present, is worthy of study as having been a help or hindrance
to human progress. But in our study of man and his en-
viroment, we must not forget an important distinction,
which is frequently overlooked. Nature, so far as
we can learn, is the product of a single system of
forces, working apparently according to a harmonious
plan. (Whether nature is the product of mere chance, of
preordained pupose, or of other Power, this is not the
place to inquire.) Man, on the other hand, according to
our previous assumption, is a center of force within a
force, a plan within a plan. His evolution is the combined product of nature and his own intelligence, and the
share of each of these forces, in the product, is at this
moment a warmly disputed question, as the recent works
of such men as Benjamin Kidd, A. E. Taylor, and others
bear evidence. I shall have more to say on the subject in a
later part of this essay; at present it will suffice to say
that in my opinion the part played by intelligence in the
development of man and human institutions has been
much larger than evolutionary philosophers are inclined
to admit. Most of our ethical concepts and beliefs, it
seems to me, are the result of the perception or the supposed perceptions of the consequences of actions. Even
our ethical emotions are to a considerable extent, altho
by no means altogether, the product of individual and
racial experience. By means of intelligence and its in-
strument, language, the individual and the society of today are the heirs of a rich estate in experience. Our concepts and beliefs have come down to us like precious heirlooms, well tested and ready for use; not, however, thro'
inherited brain and nerve tissue, but by example, training, custom, institutions, and word of mouth. This view,
I am well aware, is in opposition both to those of the intuitionists, led by such men as James Martineau and
Henry Calderwood, on the one hand, and to those of the

evolutionists, led by Herbert Spencer, A. Sutherland, and Leslie Stephen, on the other.

The intuitionists go too far in making our ethical emotions, concepts, and beliefs, purely innate or intuitive, and hence inexplicable, and not to be tampered with. On the other hand, the evolutionists go too far in trying to explain the origin of all our emotions, concepts and beliefs by means of evolution alone. While we all admit that the civilized man of today is somewhat superior to the savage of six thousand years ago in ethical emotions, yet when we reflect, on the one hand, on the immense progress in emotional and ethical development which the negro has undergone during the three hundred years of his sojourn in America, and on the other hand on the fact that the child of refined parents, thrown by chance among savages (a very common occurrence in colonial days in America) exhibits no higher ethical emotions, concepts and beliefs than his savage fellows, we are forced to the conclusion that most of the ethical emotions, concepts and beliefs are institutional in origin, that is, the results of the accumulated experience of the race, gathered and transmitted in maxims, proverbs, institutions and even in the very words of the language itself. Suppose, for instance, that a million infants were selected from the most refined homes in the world and transported to a deserted island unfrequented by men, and sustained by ravens until they were old enough to care for themselves; is it not almost certain that the children would in time become the most degraded savages? Indeed, unless the island were entirely free from noxious animals and poisonous plants, it is very probable that the whole colony would perish in a very few years. Be this as it may, I cannot conceive that the rapid development of ethical concepts in western Europe within the last few centuries could be the result of so slow a progress as evolution. Leslie Stephen, in his English Utilitarians, remarks "the sudden awakening of the public conscience"[*] in England on the slave trade just prior to the French Revolution. Before

---

[*]The Eng. Util. Vol. I, page 113-14.

that awakening, the most respectable people engaged in
the trade without a qualm of conscience. The generation
which is just passing in America can recall a like awakening here on the slave question. Even the time which has
elapsed since the days of Socrates, Plato, and Ariostotle
is not sufficient to account for the marked advance on
Grecian ethical concepts which is so strikingly depicted
in T. H. Green's Prolegomena to Ethics. Much less could
the slow progress of mental evolution account for the
wonderful changes in ethical concepts which A. Sutherland has so masterfully pictured in his Origin and Growth
of the Moral Instinct. But when we note the strides
which the sciences have made since the days of Socrates,
and particularly within the last three centuries, when we
recall the progress of the arts and of our knowledge of all
that relates to man's physical and social well-being, we need
not be surprised at the rapid changes which have taken place
in men's ethical notions. And when we reflect upon the
force of habit, the strength of custom, the tenacity of inherited beliefs, and the universal ignorance of the ultimate
foundation of institutions in general, we can only be surprised that opinions have yielded as rapidly as they have
to the wave of progress[1]. But if the evolutionists have in
their zeal gone too far in ascribing the whole of man's progress to the power of evolution, they have, until the last few
years, failed to emphasize sufficiently the importance of
the part which nature plays in developing the anti-selfish
or altruistic emotions. So far as I know, Benjamin Kidd,
in his social evolution, was the first to call attention to
this remarkable fact. I shall discuss the subject.
At present I need only say that I regard this peculiar fact,
that nature develops the race in opposition to the individual's development of himself, as one of the greatest
marvels in science and at the same time the solution of
the apparent contradiction which runs all through human
life and activity. I believe it offers the only solution of
the ethical problem, the only basis for harmonizing conflicting ethical theories. In this brief essay I can do no

[1]See Leslie Stephen, the Eng. Util. Vol. I, page 5.

more than blaze a few trees along the route, leaving
to others the work of clearing a broad highway.

1. Evolution and Ethics.

As I stated in the preliminary section, ethics was still
in need of an element in the form of evolution before it
could give a satisfactory and rational account of human
activity and conduct. So long as human instincts and
human prejudices had to be accepted as inexplicable facts,
it was impossible to distinguish instinctive and impulsive
activity from voluntary conduct. No one could gainsay
the arguments of the intuitionist, no matter how absurd
his pretensions might be. The claim of the Morman and
Mohammedan of the right to enjoy more than one wife,
the claim of the cannibal to eat his enemy, and the claim
of the hermit to the right to live an isolated life were
equally unassailable. But since evolution has pointed
out the probable origin and the growth of not only
nearly every human institution, but of the very moral
sentiments themselves, intuitionism is, in the words of
Professor Muirhead, "entirely out of court."[5] The ideas
of law and gradual development throw a new light on
every phase of human nature and human institutions.
According to the doctrine of evolution, the individual
man, as well as man the species, is the product of a
gradual development; and this development is largely
by means of natural selection through the survival of the
fittest in the struggle for existence. When the facts of the
struggle for existence are first presented to us, they are
apt to produce quite a shock to our moral feelings. The
amount of suffering involved in the process is simply
inconceivable and inexplicable. It was these facts that J.
S. Mill had in mind when he wrote his scathing essay on
Nature. The startling and yet unquestionable details
given in the first few chapters of Sutherland's Origin and
Growth of the Moral Instinct show conclusively that
nature does not have much regard for the individual.

[5]Elements of Ethics, p. 134.

She is apparenty working for the benefit of the race, and seems utterly indifferent to the sufferings and destruction of individuals. If we were permitted to judge nature from the human standpoint, it might be pretty hard to determine whether she is benevolent or malevolent.[6] But the ultimate purpose of conscious existence is still a mystery to us, unless we accept revealed religion. The problem of evil is no nearer solution than in the days of Job. It is the Pons Asinorum of theological ethics. We have no right, therefore, to judge nature by human standards. It is evident, however, that nature is gradually developing higher (in the sense of more complex) forms of animal life; and in man, the highest animal, of sentient intelligence. But the individual is short-lived, while the race continues. Consequently, one of the most difficult problems of ethics is the question: What interest has the individual in the persistence of the race? It is evident that Hedonism has no object in evading facts or denying the truth. It frankly admits, therefore, that at present the interest of the individual and that of society at large do not, so far as we can judge, exactly tally or correspond.[7] That the time will come to which Herbert Spencer looks forward, in which society will be in such perfect equilibrium that each individual will find his own greatest good in working for the greatest good of all other men is a possibility, an ideal at which the wise hedonist will aim as a final goal. But in the meantime, the individual, as the body politic, must have rules of action. We must not prepare our vehicles for the smooth tableland of human perfection till we have scaled the mountains of human frailty, ignorance and error. So far as social welfare coincides with individual welfare the question presents no difficulties. And as we show elsewhere, the margin of conflict is at present very narrow and tends gradually to disappear. Hadley says,[8] "Rat-

---

[6] See Paulsen, Introd. to Phil., p. 153.

[7] See B. Kidd, Western Civilization, Chap. II, 1; Stephen, Science of Chap. VII; Spencer, Data of Ethics, Chap. 12.

[8] Economics, p. 14.

tional egotism and rational altruism tend to coïncide."
But a margin of conflict there undoubtedly is at present.
And if the race is to be maintained, nature must some-
how win the day and compel the individual to act against
his own interest and in favor of the social interest. This,
as I show later, she does by means of the instincts and
emotions. Mr. Huxley, in his lecture on Evolution and
Ethics, insists that the "ethical process" and the "evolutionary process" are in direct conflict. Benevolence, altruistic conduct and sympathy are, according to him, in
direct contravention to the struggle for existence, which
is the evolutionary process. But I am forced to disagree
with him. (Huxley makes a recantation in the appendix
to this lecture.) The social instincts are direct products
of evolution. And so far as disinterested activity, so
called, rests on a religious sanction, it is not really disinterested, as I showed above.

The practical difficulty raised by Nietzsche and his
followers is much more serious. Are we to let the sympathetic impulses act to the extent of reversing the work of
evolution and preventing the survival of the fittest?
Our institutions for preserving the weak, the defective,
and the degenerate certainly make the question of serious
importance, especially as the religious and ethical
opinions of the present day tend to encourage the sentiment in favor of the preservation of the classes which
would otherwise perish.⁹ Taylor points out the difficulty
referred to above and calls it the "Paradox of Benevolence." (See below the problem of altruism.) The only
answer which Hedonism can give, aside from one based
on religious doctrines, is that nature must solve the
question for herself. Our sentiments for the weak may be
illogical, but they are facts; and Hedonism sticks to the
facts of human nature. Nor does it seem possible to
reason ourselves away from these sentiments, even if we
disregard religion. Huxley insists as strongly on the
validity of the ethical process as do Benjamin Kidd and
Dr. Martineau.

⁹See R. A. Taylor, Prob. of Conduct, p. 272 et seq.

But while the Hedonist admits that social welfare and individual welfare do not precisely tally, he denies that there is any serious decrepancy between them even at present. The apparent discrepancies are largely due to our ignorance either of the real welfare of the society or that of the individual. Only too often in the past, the welfare of the individual has been sacrificed to the supposed welfare of the state. So wise a philospher as Aristotle, for example, seemed to think that slavery is a part of the plan of nature. He did not think that slaves could be dispensed with until shuttles ceased to be thrown. Nearly every nation, past and present, has put more or less restraint upon the women. Yet those nations which have put confidence in her find that most, if not all, the restraints of the past were uncalled for. Perhaps in no distant age the enforced military service of today will seem as barbarous to those nations that still practice it as the crudities of the feudal system now seems to expert political scientists. On the other hand, the welfare of the state has been at times as clearly sacrificed to the supposed rights of the individual. For example, when the individual was allowed to be lord of his own domain to the extent of making it a place for germs of disease to grow and spread; or when each parent was left to educate or not educate his children as he saw fit; or when favored individuals were allowed to monopolize the land, water, or other means of producing a living.[10] Only in recent years have the laws of social growth and decay been studied in a truly scientific way. And what a fund of information has already been brought to light. The works of Sohm, Mommsen and others on Roman history and institutions; the works of Maine, Spencer, Tyler and others in England, and Wundt, Waitz and others in Germany on the early history and institutions of mankind generally; and the special works on sociology and social evolution of Spencer, Kidd, Lombroso and others

---

[10] These lines were written before the great coal strike of 1902 in Pennsylvania brought this particular instance strongly before the mind of everyone.

demonstrate beyond any possible doubt how small a
share the men in the past had in their own development,
or rather, how unconscious a share. For nature requires
every creature to work out his own salvation. She
neither increases nor dimishes the effects of a creature's
own acts. She establishes the laws of progress, and those
who conform to them will survive; the rest will perish.
It is not my purpose, however, to show why the laws of
nature are as they are, but rather to point out what some
of them are. Those who wish to see nature rebuked may
read J. S. Mill's essay on Nature, those on the other hand
who wish to hear her praises sounded may read their
Bridgewater Treatise, their Emerson or their Spencer.
The Hedonist prefers to accept the laws of nature as facts
and to spend his strength in adapting himself to those
laws.

This much then is certain; before man could become a
social creature, Nature must have developed in him a
social impulse or social pleasure strong enough to over-
come his objections to yielding up the liberties he could
enjoy as an independent individual. But these liberties
could not conceivably have been either very great or very
valuable. The primitive man had almost nothing to
gain, and very much to lose by living alone. But as
society gradually advances, numerically, economically,
and otherwise, the margin of temptation to evade the
requirements of social order would naturally increase.
There must be a corresponding increase, therefore, in the
social cohesiveness. Mere increase of experience and
reasoning power would, perhaps, only increase the temp-
tations of the individual to evade the social law. Nature
filled the breach by preserving the individuals who were
slightly more gifted with the social impulse or pleasure.
Thus generation after generation, little by little nature
built up man's sympathetic nature. Much of it she built
up for him no doubt, before he became man at all. For
we find the social and domestic instincts well developed in
many of the lower animals.[11] Primitive man had still a

---

[11]Sutherland, Origin and Growth of the Moral Instinct, Vol. I.

vast amount of social impulse and sympathy to develop before he could live in large societies, under elaborate institutions. But this is not the place to pursue this subject further. Those who wish to read a full discussion of the subject of the origin and growth of the moral instincts are referred to the elaborate as well as interesting work of Sutherland. My wish is only to show the attitude of Hedonism toward nature and her laws. The man with whom ethics has to deal is not, therefore, a purely self-centered being. His very constitution makes him to a greater or less extent interested in the welfare of his fellow beings. If this were not so, mankind would never have been drawn into group life.

2. The Canon of Consequences.

Every ethical theory must sooner or later find itself driven to answer the question, What constitutes the morality of an act? Wherein does one act differ from another? Why may I do this and not do that? The terms, "Ought," "Right," "Good," "Approval" and their opposites imply the existence of an answer to these questions. Many answers may have been given to the above questions. One group of moralists state in effect that the morality of an act is something ultimate, eternal, immutable and inexplicable; that right and wrong are like right and left, up and down, round and square. Those who give this answer become hopelessly confused when we ask them how they know what acts fall in one class and what in the other. The well known conflict in the actual judgments of men as to the classification of acts morally, proves conclusively that we have no sense or intuition which will infallibly guide us in this matter. And even if such a sense actually existed in each of us, we might still question its authority as a guide to action. I might still say: granted that intuition tells me this act is what you call right, yet why must I perform it! Thus the intuitionist must at last fall back on some more ultimate reason for his ethical classification. This is usually done by saying the right act is so commanded by God. But this assertion still permits me to ask, Why must I obey the

will or command of my fellow men, or my own will? The
only conclusive answer to this query is that God has
power to reward me if I obey, and punish me if I disobey,
and will do so. That answer gives the terms right and
wrong and intelligible, because sentient, content.

Another group of moralists, at whose head is Imman-
uel Kant, answer the ultimate ethical question by saying
that the morality of an act is its fitness to become a
universal law or maxim of conduct. A moral act is one
which we can wish anybody and everybody to perform.
But it is evident that this answer is purely formal. We
must still experience the various consequences of the
various kinds of acts before we can say whether we are
willing for all men to perform them.[12] In other words, we
must fall back on the consequences of actions. Those
acts which benefit us we will want other men to perform.
Those acts which pain or injure us we shall want them to
omit.[13]

Another group of moralists argue that the morality
of an act lies in its tendency to promote the perfection of
an action. But the term "perfection" is empty until we
have formed an idea of perfection. Perfection relates
rather to the means than to the end.[14] The means are
perfect when they are best adapted to accomplish the
given design or purpose. Perhaps we are not yet pre-
pared to define the perfect man; but a tentative definition
must certainly include his sentient nature, that is, his
capacity to suffer and enjoy; the perfect man will be least
subject to pain and best equipped for enjoyment. Those,
such as Dr. Paul Carus,[15] who make work the ideal of
conduct overlook the fact that work is a means, not an
end. I, as a free creature, live, keep healthly, and work,
for the sake of carrying out my ideal. The work, the life,
and the health themselves I care nothing about. It is the
fullest sentient consciousness that I desire; and because

---

[12]See Caird, Crit. Philos. of Kant, II. p. 290.

[13]Taylor, op. cit., p. 351.

[14]Alexander, Moral Order and Progress, p. 190.

[15]The Ethical Problem, 2nd ed.

life, health and work make this possible, I care for them as
means.[16] Experience reveals to us the laws of cause and
effect, the unity of Nature and the conservation of force.
The whole universe, so far as we know it, is subject to
universal laws. Man, along with his fellow animals,
has been developed from lower creatures by means of the
natural selection of advantageous variations in form and
character (together with other forces yet unknown, no
doubt). After the appearance of intelligence and volition,
animals have some share in the shaping of their own lives.
Man has far outstriped his fellow animals in intelligence,
as to memory, power of attention, observation, association of ideas and reason. With the dawn of reason, man
began to observe the consequences of his actions. Those
actions which conduced to his pleasure or preservation,
and especially to the latter, were repeated. Those men
who were luckiest in hitting upon the most preservative
acts succeeded in the race for existence, (or rather persistence) while their less fortunate neighbors perished.
As intelligence continued to develop, men began to study
the consequences of their actions with more care. In time
certain consequences became so well known that every
man knew how to bring them about and they were
accepted as a matter of course. But there was always a
margin, and a large margin of acts the utility of whose
consequences was disputed. Men could not agree as to
whether these acts should be done or not. This was
especially true of acts whose consequences were complex
or remote. But whenever the consequences, (that is, the
aggressive or approximately total consequences) of an
act were well known or supposed to be known, men generally agreed as to its morality, that is, as to whether it
should be done or omitted. The desired consequences
have usually been the escape from bodily or mental pain,
from disease, suffering and torment, in this life and the
next, as might be within reach. A study of the actual
systems of morality and the actual desires, fears, hopes
and ambitions of men, past and present, will, I believe,

---

[16]Taylor, Problem of Conduct, p. 353.

show the correctness of this analysis. The consequences of an act, in terms of pleasure and pain, are and must be the ultimate criterion of its morality or permissibility. Any other criterion must, sooner or later, resolve itself into this one. Every formal criterion of activity must have a content of sentience before it is of any practical value. A sentient consciousness is never satisfied with a formal answer to the query, Why must I do this? But an answer in terms of pleasure and pain gives immediate and complete satisfaction. When I direct an intelligent creature not to do a thing because the consequences of doing it are thus and so, he can determine for himself whether I have pointed out a sufficient sanction for the law I have asserted. I trespass neither on his freedom of judgment nor on his freedom of action. The law is not categorical or imperative. It is disjunctive. Each person may determine for himself whether to accept or reject the consequences of an act.

This Hedonism, which is based on the canon of consequences, is the only logical doctrine of ethics.

3. The Province of Intelligence.

One more point and I shall have finished the outline of what I regard as the essentials of Hedonism. I have pointed out that most of the human suffering and error of the past was the result of ignorance and imperfection. We have further seen that even the well-meant efforts of men acting together in society to better their condition have very often produced the reverse of the intended effects. The question will now occur: Would it not be better to abandon ourselves entirely to the care of nature, and not attempt to guide men by human laws and human institutions? More than one leading thinker has advocated such a course. Long before any one thought of applying the laws of evolution to the growth of society, Rousseau proposed that men should go back to a state of nature. Many of the leading economists of the last century advocated to some extent a similar view in their "laissez faire" doctrine. Even Herbert Spencer and his followers take the same position, apparently, at times when denouncing the legislation of the past and present. But after all, men's disposition to form these institutions is also a natural disposition, and a wise second thought shows us that, in spite of all his mistakes, the man of today has survived by means of his institutions. Those tribes and races whose laws and institutions were anti-social decayed and disappeared; while those who were fortunate enough or wise enough to adopt beneficial institutions and laws survived and progressed.

The mere fact of survival shows that the peoples that survived had either internal or external qualities, or both combined, that enabled them to outstrip their competitors in the race for existence. The latter alternative seems the more probable: there was a combination of mental traits and external institutions which carried the victorious races to the goal. But this does not amount to the assertion that existing institutions cannot be improved upon. Other institutions might have been devised which would have proved infinitely superior to those actually adopted. Had the Athenians, for example, with all their intellectual keenness, their artistic insight and their executive ability, devised a form of federal government similar to that of the United States at the present day, or had they even developed the genius for law and government which the ancient Romans manifested, no one can say to what degree of civilization they might have attained. Or had the Chinese in the days of Confucius combined with their industry, sobriety and inventive cleverness the flexibility of character which encourages change and progress, they, too, might have become a world power. Going still further back into the past, had the ancient Egyptians combined with their marvelous mechanical skill, their architectural talent and their knowledge of the sciences of geography, astronomy and writing the inclination to educate the whole people instead of a favored class, and the disposition to build monuments economically useful instead of pyramids and spynxes, they, too, might still be the leading nation of the world. But what has been, has been; our business is to study the past for the purpose of improving the future.

We have much to learn from the attempt of past generations to solve the problems of conduct, both individual and social. And we may profit as much, if not more, by their mistakes than by their successes. The science of government is yet far from perfect; it will continue to present new difficulties to each succeeding generation. But men who can live peaceably together in societies aggregating from 50,000,000 to 100,000,000 are surely much in advance of savages who straggle about in groups of from ten to fifty. The institutions of the larger groups are, to a very great extent, based on dear-bought experience. They are the result of the accumulated experience and wisdom of the past. By means of language, oral and written, each generation was able to start nearly where the preceding left off. The wisdom of the group is infinitely beyond that of any of the individuals composing it. For the division of labor and knowledge make it impossible as well as unnecessary and unprofitable for any one man to carry all the knowledge of the age in his head. One must not be too positive, however, touching the social value of any institution. The laws of social existence and progress are so complex that we can only make provisional statements concerning any institution and wait for time to demonstrate whether we are correct or not. The germs of destruction may be developing in institutions which we look upon as the most precious. It follows, then, that both nature and intelligence must take part in the evolution of human destiny. Much of the work only nature can perform. But there is also a place for intelligence, for human reason and endeavor. If I had time, it would be easy to show that Mr. Sutherland, in his otherwise excellent book,[17] has committed the fault of overlooking the share of intelligence, as taught by experience, in altering human institutions and human ways of looking at things and conduct.[18] But I cannot agree with the conclusion of Taylor that biological evolution would not have carried

---

[17] The Origin and Growth of Moral Instinct.
[18] See the strong statement of Taylor, Prob. of Conduct, p. 235 et seq.

the human race beyond the agricultural stage. Nature is not satisfied with the mere maintenance of the race. The law of evolution still holds good, and those individuals who happen to be more sympathetic and to derive more pleasure from sympathetic activity will tend to survive the less sympathetic. Thus self-interest and social interest will tend, through natural selection, to become identical.[19]

It is the dawning perception of the relation of things that changes our opinions as to the value of conduct, and not, as Mr. Sutherland insists, altogether the evolution of sympathy in us by the secret force of nature.[20]

Whatever Hedonism may have meant, therefore, in the days of Aristippus and Epicurus, in the days of Hobbes and Locke, or even in the days of Jeremy Bentham and the two Mills, at the present day evolutionary Hedonism, when it is careful not to fall into the vice of mere mechanism, means that each of us has the right to the fullest realization of himself which is consistent with the same right on the part of other intelligent beings;[21] that as man is not only a conscious but also a sentient, or pleasure-pain creature, he is entitled to the fullest development of his whole nature; that pleasure and health or welfare go hand in hand, while pain is the index of disorder, maladjustment, lack of equilibrium, or decay; that pain in itself can never be a good; at most it can only be the negative means of leading to something else as a good or end;[22] while pleasure, if not the end itself, is at least the inseparable accompaniment of the end, and in the long run the only safe criterion to the end; that nature (which may mean the Creator acting through nature if you like) takes care of intelligent creatures by means of instincts and impulses until their reason is sufficiently developed to perceive the purpose of pain and pleasure in the economy of life and their knowledge sufficiently great to realize the laws of nature and their rela-

[19]See Huxley, Evolution and Ethics, Note 20, p. 114.
[20]Stephen, op. cit., p. 103.
[21]Spencer, Prin. Ethics, p. 46.
[22]Alexander, Moral Order, etc., p. 225.

tion to the sentient creature. Hedonism takes man as
the partially developed product of evolution and seeks to
show him as an individual and as a race what possibilities nature has in store for him; and if there be an after
life, how the present life may be best lived as a preliminary to that. Hedonism is obliged to draw upon all the
other sciences for its material.²³ In fact all the sciences
are but the more or less systematic efforts of man to find
his place in the universe.²⁴ Among the sciences which
Hedonism will draw most from are the sciences of the
human body, its health and ailments, the economic
sciences, or the sciences of satisfying man's needs, and the
political and legal sciences, or the sciences which govern
man's actions in society. For evolutionary Hedonism
recognizes that man is by nature a sociable creature;
that each tribe, nation or people, in fact, is a sort of
organism, subject to definite laws of growth and decay.
The welfare of the individual is, therefore, largely a function of the organism of which he is a part; thus while a
wise man like Socrates or Confucius might be happy
among miserable associates he could be much happier, if
his associates were also wiser and happier. Altruism, or
interest in the welfare of others, is thus to a large extent an element of Hedonism.

III.   The Strength of Hedonism.

The chief theory of conduct which is opposed to
Hedonism is intuitionism, the theory of duty or conscience. This theory looks to the human sentiments for a
basis for activity. We are to be guided in our actions,
not by their experienced consequences on ourselves and
others, but by the approving or disapproving voice of
this inward monitor.

Without stopping to inquire at present into the
origin and nature of this inward monitor, we find on
investigation that it has varied enormously in different
ages, races, localities and individuals. Thus we find that
slavery has met with almost universal approval in times

---

²³Paulsen, System of Ethics, Introd.
²⁴Weber, Hist. Philos., p. 1.

past, being recognized in the sacred books of the Hebrews, Hindus, Chinese, Greeks and Egyptians, and being practiced to a greater or less extent by all nations. At the present time it is condemned by nearly all civilized men. The subjection of women has been likewise generally approved and practiced. Only in the most recent times and among the most developed nations has woman begun to receive the same treatment as man. Even at the present day our sense of duty does not urge us to give her the same political and social rights that men possess. Custom keeps her wages lower than those of men engaged in precisely the same work.[25] Again, the sense of duty has not prevented the basest treatment and neglect of children, even among people who were the most scrupulous, such as the Puritans.

Once more, the caste system prevails among a large proportion of mankind. The sense of duty not only does not require members of the higher caste to treat those of a lower caste as their equals, but on the contrary positively forbids such treatment. Nor is the caste system by any means confined to Asia. The young woman who marries below her station in Europe or America loses caste almost as surely as does the Hindu belle. The very word friendship implies a broader form of selfishness. One is expected to do for a friend what he would not do for a stranger or an enemy. Our consciences call on us to help a friend who is in trouble; while they are not much stirred by the sufferings of Hindus and Chinese, unless their sufferings become widespread and excessive. The word patriotism likewise implies that our country is to be preferred to other countries. Even if we do not accept the maxim, "Our country, right or wrong," we are apt to be strongly biased in her favor in case of rivalry or conflict with other countries.

In opposition to the above illustrations,[26] Paul Janet and others seek to demonstate a general uniformity of opinion in all ages and nations on moral questions. But

---

[25] See Report of Com. of Labor, Vol. XI.
[26] Theory of Morals, Bk. III, ch. 4.

the cases cited by them seem to show simply that the
universal reasoning and sentient, pleasure-pain faculties
of mankind have led them gradually to learn the same
facts regarding human and physical nature, and to adapt
themselves to these facts. The activities necessary to
maintain the individual and the race, after making the
necessary allowances for differences in the environment,
must be more or less similar everywhere; and if men desire
to live in society, certain general and evident rules of conduct must be established and followed. But beyond these
apparent and fundamental cases, it seems impossible to
harmonize the moral views of mankind. For in
addition to the cases of conflicting consciences
which we have already given, we have other
cases of a much more radical kind. In the sexual re-
lations we find differences in opinion the most remote. To
say nothing of monogamy, polygamy and polyandry, such
writers as Spencer, Westermark and Sutherland give
instances of what we regard as looseness of sexual practice, which are almost inconceivable. So in matters of
honesty and veracity, we find that among many nations,
honesty and veracity are not supposed to be due to a
foreigner. Theft from a stranger and even from a neighbor was applauded not only in ancient Sparta, but in
many other countries. And even in civilized countries
clever dishonesty and deception are too often approved
where the parties are very unequally situated: for
example when one outwits and cheats an employer, a
great corporation, or the public officers. There is often a
feeling of approval of the clever urchin, who deceives his
teacher. And I have heard old soldiers of high standing
tell with evident self-satisfaction how they deceived and
defrauded their officers, and their stories were approved
by their audience. The most intelligent people sometimes
will be found to distinguish between lying and deceit.
Many a man who would suffer torture rather than lie
verbally, will not hesitate to deceive by actions.[27]

But a closer examination shows us that the sense of

---

[27]See H. Spencer, Ethics II, §156; also The Outlook, Vol. 73, p. 262-3.

duty, or conscience is exceedingly compliant and flexible.
It gives way in nearly every instance to the accepted
religious code. Whatever is prescribed by the accepted
religion is approved by the sense of duty. This accounts
for the child-murders so common among heathen tribes.
The tribes of ancient Palestine laid their infants in the
red-hot arms of a metallic god. The Hindu mother
throws her babe to the crocodile and even Abraham was
ready to sacrifice his only son at the supposed call of
deity. But the sense of duty bends not only at the dictate of religion, but at the dictate of custom, where
custom and religion do not conflict. Hence the most
absurd costumes are worn, the most absurd rites
observed, and the most absurd practices maintained,
simply because custom has established them. In this case
the sense of duty requires one to respect public opinion.
This opinion is vastly stronger among the uncivilized
than among ourselves. But even the best of us feel
impelled by the sense of duty to comply with the customs
in force around us.

Once more, the sense of duty usually complies with the
existing laws, in so far as they do not conflict with our
religious beliefs.

In any age and nation, therefore, we may expect to
find the general conscience or sense of duty pretty clearly
defined by the prevailing religious code, together with the
accepted customs and political laws in force. If the religion is false and maintains pernicious rites and doctrines,
the sense of duty will be accordingly perverted. If the
customs are absurd and injurious, the political laws illogical and narrow, the keener intellects will probably strive
very gradually to modify them in the direction of
improving the social welfare, but the sense of duty of the
multitude will always lag far in the rear of the car of
progress. For progress is usually the work of a select
few; and the multitude are very slow to perceive the
advantages of a change in well established institutions.[28]

We are forced to the conclusion, therefore, that the

---

[28]See Bryce, Studies in Hist. and Jurist.—Obedience, p. 463.

sense of duty, or conscience is not a safe and sufficient guide to human conduct.

The sentiments play an extremely important part in human affairs; but we cannot safely rely on them as the ultimate criterion of the rectitude of an action or course of conduct. What habit does for one in matters of bodily action, the sentiments do for him in matters of volition. Habit permits us to devote the mind to other matters while the body carries out a given line of conduct. So the sentiments dispense with the necessity of going back to first principles before deciding on every act. They are moral habits, nothing more.

If, then, intuitionism, with its reliance on an inward monitor, is unable to provide an ultimate basis for human activity, a philosophy of conduct, what has Hedonism to offer in its stead? Wherein lies the strength of Hedonism? We must admit at the start that Hedonism has a bad name. Any doctrine which advocates selfishness must expect to be frowned upon. And among Christian peoples, at any rate, any doctrine based on pleasure must likewise expect to meet strong opposition. Unless, therefore, the Hedonist can make out a strong and clear case in its favor, he must not expect any mercy at the hands of his opponents and critics. More than this, I realize only too clearly that a misunderstood theory of pleasure might cause a vast deal of harm. It would perhaps be better to let men blunder along after their old guides than to have them think they need no guide at all; that they are at liberty to do as they please, and to gratify every desire and passion as it arises. It is incumbent on the Hedonist to guard by every possible precaution against any such misconception of his doctrine. Hedonism, as I understand the doctrine, seeks to establish a philosophical basis for conduct, not a stronghold for the libertine. It is not intended to work any sudden revolution in the morals and manners of civilized men, and this for the simple reason that in spite of their erroneous theories of the ultimate bases of conduct and of certain details of activity, civilized peoples have unconsciously followed hedonistic principles in their development. They have

builded better than they knew. The canon of consequences has been accepted and followed to some extent in
all ages and nations. But other theories have often
greatly retarded its application, even to the extent of
destroying great nations. The nations which have survived and progressed are, I believe, those which have
grasped most firmly and applied most faithfully the canon
of consequences. As I have tried to point out in the first
section, it was largely because the ancient Greeks were
untrammelled by any religious code that they were able to
make the freest use of the canon of consequences. Thus
they were able to develop the most accurate and valuable
moral theory which the world knew before the present
age, and by its use to reach the highest pinnacle of civilization. I cannot agree with Mr. Spencer in his indictment
of Greek civilization.[29] The Hindu and the Chinaman, on
the contrary, tied themselves hand and foot with strin-
gent religious and social codes.

Hedonism, therefore, is evolutionary, rather than
revolutionary. It conceives that there are vastly higher
and broader stages of civilization yet in store for humanity; but it does not hope to attain these by any sudden
leap. It will have done enough if it enables the car of
civilization to move steadily onward and upward.

Yet at the present time, when the ethical problem,
that is, the question as to the ultimate foundation of
moral conduct, is studied and discussed as it never was
before, it seems well worth while to help all one can in
reaching a solution of the problem.

In the first place, then, Hedonism is irreconcilably
opposed to every form of asceticism, that is, to pain for
the sake of pain. Nearly all the religious and ethical
systems of the past have been vitiated by the taint of
asceticism. This is not the place to inquire into the
origin of the monstrous notion that the Deity could take
delight in the sufferings of his creatures. It is sufficient
for our purpose to call attention to the important place
which this belief occupies in most religious systems. The

---

[29] Ethics, II, § 58.

religious and ethical systems of western Asia and Europe seem to have drawn their ascetic element from Egypt, where, according to Schaff,[20] a pessimistic atmosphere seems always to have prevailed. Christianity has not escaped the taint. In spite of the humane teachings of Jesus, the Egyptian influence was strong enough to fill the symbols of the church with ascetic doctrines and all Europe with monks and monasteries.

Hedonism insists that men have a right to be happy, that pain is intended to benefit and not to torture, that the religious or ethical doctrine demanding suffering or sacrifice that does not result in a greater compensating good to the sufferer or some other sentient creature, is certainly erroneous.

Asceticism is unreasonable and cannot justify itself. Yet the ascetic element in various guises is really what makes most other ethical systems different from Hedonism. Thus it is this element of asceticism which, sometimes drawing strength from the doctrine of self-discipline or stoicism, constitutes the essence of all the doctrines of despair, such as Buddhism. The ethics of despair may be hedonistic if it avoids this ascetic element. For if the powers of evil really are stronger in the universe, then doubtless we are justified in seeking Nirvana or some other escape into non-existence. But we are still at liberty to reinvestigate the facts of nature for the purpose of deciding whether existence is on the whole too painful to be endurable. There was but little of the ascetic element in the stoicism of Greece and Rome. But when the current of orientalism struck the philosophy of Greece, the ascetic element mingled with the philosophic and pain for the sake of pain became a prominent element in the ethical doctrines of the middle ages.

Preserved by the religious orders against the strong reaction of German common sense which swept over western Europe with the spread of German civilisation, asceticism sprang again into prominence at the reformation in the Puritanism of England and Germany. During

---

[20] Church History.

the last three centuries men have been gradually elimi-
nating the ascetic element from the religious and ethical
systems of Europe. The reaction probably reached flood
tide in the days of William Paley and Jeremy Bentham.
Since their day there has been a slight disposition to
revert toward asceticism, owing partly to the writings of
Thomas Carlyle and partly to disappointment of the
hopes placed in the political and social reforms of the
nineteenth century.

Asceticism draws a certain amount of strength from
the evident value of self-discipline. But asceticism, or
pain for its own sake, and self-discipline, or pain for the
sake of compensating good to self or others are radically
different. Self-discipline is a hedonistic doctrine. Experience teaches the value of discipline as clearly as it teaches
the absurdity of asceticism. But too often the one is
taken for the other. Suffering to produce good for
another is confused with suffering that another is supposed to enjoy as suffering. It is a curious fact in nature
that sentient creatures are unquestionably able to enjoy
the agony of their fellow creatures. By a natural infer-
ence, one's deity is supposed to possess this same abnormal characteristic. But of all illogical and abhorrent
emotions, this one seems to be unquestionably the worst.
Hedonism insists that no being, be he creator or creature,
has the right to enjoy the pain of another.

Whatever destiny the powers of the universe have in
store for me, I have certainly the right, in so far as I have
the power, to make that destiny as little painful and as
fully pleasant as possible. And the same right which I
insist upon for myself, I insist upon with equal emphasis
for my fellowmen.

In the next place, Hedonism is the natural doctrine of
conduct. All sentient creatures seek pleasure and avoid
pain as naturally and as certainly as water seeks its level.
Indeed, the tendency to seek pleasure and avoid pain is so
strong and natural that an opposite doctrine seems
almost inconceivable. Hence not only many philosophers
but even whole nations, as the Hindus, believe that sentience and activity are inseparably connected by the law of

cause and effect. But without admitting this extreme view, we must concede a natural disposition or tendency in all conscious beings to seek pleasure and avoid pain. Moreover, science seems to indicate that pleasure and pain are teleological, that is, they play an important part in the preservation and evolution of both the individual and the race. No one will deny that without the faculties of pleasure and pain no living creature could maintain its existence very long. Sentience, or pleasure-pain is the faculty which enables a living creature to maintain the equilibrium with its environment which is essential to life. And pleasure, usually, if not always indicates that the equilibrium is satisfactory, while pain, usually, if not always, indicates that something is wrong. If one were disposed to argue, therefore, that man is the creation of an intelligent being, the existence of these wise provisions for his persistence among the struggling forces of the universe would certainly be a strong point in his favor. But whether the gift of an intelligent Creator, or the product of chance, pleasure and pain are certainly indispensible faculties of all sentient creatures. And even if we can never demonstrate that conscious existence was intended to be as pleasant as possible, or that the individual may strive to make it as pleasant as possible, we are at least certain that without the pleasure-pain apparatus, conscious creatures could not subsist at all. Pleasure being, then, such an inseparable accompaniment of healthy, normal consciousness, and pain as clearly the index of the abnormal and defective, is not the burden on the opponents of Hedonism to show that sentience should not be taken as the ultimate guide to conduct? As we have repeatedly indicated above, sentience alone would not be a sufficient guide to conduct, from the fact that man is an exceedingly complex being, full of conflicting desires and emotions. Reason, therefore, must stand as judge among the pleasure-pains and determine which are entitled to recognition as components of the sum total of pleasurable consciousness and which should be rejected as injurious to the sentient community.

To the question: Why has Hedonism a bad name? we answer: Because men see that the pleasure seeker so often comes to grief and makes himself and others miserable. Ignorance and folly too often misguide men in the search for happiness. Hence the advocate of Hedonism cannot repeat too frequently that sentience alone cannot be relied upon as a guide to conduct. But neither must this statement be misconstrued or misquoted. For after all, reason must rely on sentience as the test. But it is the course of sentience, the sum of pleasures or whatever one may call the total make-up and summary of a complete conscious existence, considering both its quality, or breadth, its intensity or depth and its duration or length which reason must direct and govern. The reader will see the difficulty of translating sentient ideas into terms of space and quantity. Yet I doubt not that he will understand what I mean. Another reason for this ill-repute of Hedonism is the fact that it is often mistakenly supposed to be opposed to self-restraint and self-discipline. But philosophic Hedonism, as we have said again and again, is in the fullest accord with all legitimate self-discipline. If we always remember therefore that the aim and end of Hedonism is to secure the richest, fullest, deepest, purest, longest, pleasant consciousness for the individual, we shall not be confused or misled by instances of blind and foolish pleasure-seeking, with their calamitous and repulsive results nor by any unfair comparisons with self-disciplining ethical regimes. Every sentient creature desires pleasure, or happiness as well as escape from pain and evil. Hedonism endeavors to help him obtain these results in the fullest degree, it may be by self-restraint or it may be by self-culture or indulgence. It does not tell men: You must do thus and so; it simply says: If you wish a given result you may obtain it in a certain way. The man who breaks the law of hedonism will call himself a fool. And most men would rather be anything else than fools.

Hedonism, then, is the only natural ethics, the only ethics which seeks to lead and guide men rather than drive them, the only ethics which appeals to both their emotions and their reason, their whole nature, instead of commanding and compelling them.

But man is by nature a social creature. He prefers with the ant and many higher animals to live in groups. And the greater his development and intelligence the larger become the groups in which he lives. But group-life, or social-life is only possible under certain conditions and only enjoyable to those endowed with the social or sympathetic emotions. The individual must consent to give up certain pleasures and liberties, must submit to certain rules and restraints. I care not whether you prefer Hobbes' theory of the Original State of War, which drove reasonable men into society as the lesser of two evils, or Rousseau's theory of the Social Contract, entered into by mutual consent for the sake of its advantages, or the theory of a divinely instituted state with the place of each member eternally fixed for him, or the theory of a state slowly evolved by natural processes. The result is the same in the end. Social life means the yielding up of certain liberties and pleasures by the individual which he might enjoy if he lived alone, and the acquisition of certain joys and comforts which the anchorite must forego.

Hedonism can be applied to several of these political theories. But in any given society the thoughtful individual submits to the social law, be it political, economical or etiquetical, because the advantages to himself of such submission are greater than the disadvantages. I am aware that the multitude submit to social rules largely from the force of habit, indolence, reverence, fear and affection.[31] But even the most ignorant man has a vague idea of the reasons for social laws. The most stupid man has an occasional brilliant idea, and the ferment of ideas in the multitude will in time seize upon the beneficial social principles and throw out the defective ones, much as the fermentation of cider throws extraneous matter to the top of the cask. The popular wisdom is thus not

---

[31]See Bryce, Studies, etc., IX Obedience, and X, The Nature of Sovereignty.

entirely to be despised, especially among a progressive people.

Hedonism, then, is the logical basis of all prudent conduct, whether in the pursuit of knowledge, of health and comfort, of family affairs, of friendly intercourse with our neighbors, of art and culture, or in the greater intercourse which makes up the nation and the family of nations. There can never be any conflict between Hedonism and the sciences and arts. All the sciences and arts are the hand-maidens of Hedonism. Whatever makes men wiser, stronger, healthier, richer, more industrious, more friendly, more practical and enduring, better trained and educated for the struggle with nature, their environment and their own character will be welcomed by the hedonist. Whatever on the other hand, makes men ignorant, weak, sickly, poor, lazy, ill-natured, stupid, boorish, narrow, mean, unfriendly, harsh, reckless or in any other way retards progress and enlightenment is condemned by Hedonism. Nor is there anything inconsistent in this position. In case of the drunkard and the opium fiend, everybody can see the folly of his course of action. But in these other cases of a narrow selfishness or willfulness, the perversity and disadvantage of the course is only not so apparent. Every man desires health and strength, vigor and skill. If men disregard the laws of health, therefore, it is either through ignorance or though a weakness of the will brought on by various causes. Even while indulging the craving for drink or for morphine the drunkard does not cease to regret the probably ultimate results of his folly. It is the business of Hedonism to persuade men to discipline themselves not for the sake of discipline, nor to gratify the whim of a superior, but for their own good and greater pleasure in the end.

If every man has an equal right to seek happiness in his own way, certain logical results follow which it is important to consider in this place. In the first place, it follows that in one sense might makes right. A man may do what he likes and what he can. But other men may do the same; and it follows that by combination the superior number may restrain the inferior. But if we were to stop here Hedonism would be the most pernicious of all doctrines. We hasten to add, therefore, with the apostle, that all things are not expedient. What one may do, and what, all things considered, he will prefer to do are very different. Thus, it is in my power to destroy my furniture, to mistreat my dog and my child, to be harsh with my wife and surly with my friends; but experience teaches me that these things are not expedient. And if my nature has been properly developed, they are undesirable and repugnant to me. Kindness, affection and friendliness pay better in the long run. Hedonism urges men, therefore, to the most careful study of the whole situation. Right is not what one is able to do, but rather what one who is normally developed prefers to do and must do to attain his greatest welfare, that is, his fullest sentient consciousness.

It also follows from the principle of the equal right of all to strive for their own greatest good, that each man may join in the restraint of his fellow-men where their actions interfere with his welfare. But this doctrine is also likely to be misunderstood. As stated above, it is an empty formula. The individual should still inquire into ultimate results. Such an inquiry, the Hedonist claims, will show that the welfare of the normal individual is nearly always identical with that of the group. Admitting that there are rare cases where social welfare and individual welfare appear not to coincide as the world and the individual are now made up, yet the hedonist insists that in the long run the good of the state and that of the individual are identical. Thus utilitarianism is a branch of Hedonism. For in striving for the greatest good of the greatest number (the formula of utilitarianism), the individual feels sure that indirectly he is promoting his own welfare.

It will readily be seen from what has already been said that Hedonism is not only superior to other ethical systems in its appeal to men's natural inclinations and

emotions, but that it has the advantage of appealing to
their reason and experience as well, and is thus the only
progressive ethics. A moral system which rests on men's
sentiments, on custom or on some vague metaphysical principle, such as the doctrine of the everlasting and immutable right, tends to become more and more rigid and
stationary. Thus the Hindus, with their complicated Brah-
minical law, are shut off from all opportunity of advance
in civilization. The Chinese, likewise, with the Confucian
doctrines and customary morality have been stationary
in civilization for two thousand years. The ancient Jew,
through a misinterpretation of the Mosaic law, or a
defect in that law, was excluded from all progress in art
and culture. So during the middle ages theological ethics
hindered the progress of art, science and commerce in endless ways. Who can say how much higher civilization
would be now if women had enjoyed the same freedom
since the beginning of the christian era that they enjoy in
America today?

These instances will show the importance of having a
moral principle which encourages instead of retarding
science and culture. That other moral theories have constructed lofty ideals, the hedonist is ready enough to
admit. Buddha, Confucius, Zarathustra, and Kant were
all high-minded and noble men. But in so far as they
based their moral systems on false principles, they were
the means of retarding rather than improving the condition of the people.

Buddhism is rich in noble maxims of conduct. But as
a whole it is probably worse that no system at all.
Zarathustra and Confucius taught many wholesome doctrines, but taken as a whole, their systems have retarded
civilization.

So the formalism of Kant might be safe enough in an
age where each of the virtues had a well settled, practical
meaning for the individual; and where the duty to
parents, to children, to neighbors and to the state were
well recognized. But the fact that they were settled
would make change all the more difficult if any formal
theory of ethics were adopted. "So act that the maxim

of your conduct may be adopted as a universal law" becomes dangerous among a people who are settled in their customs. For, as was pointed out above, the sentiments of the individual are almost certain to approve the existing regime. And when a more vigorous thinker appears, who sees the injurious effects in terms of welfare, of existing practices, he meets with universal opposition from all the advocates of formalism.

In the next place, we notice that Hedonism is not only the natural, logical and progressive ethics. We find that it has been the actual element of value in all the great ethical systems of the past. From the very awakening of intelligence, sentient, conscious beings must have begun to study the consequences of actions, along with the laws of nature and of the human constitution. Conduct which is guided by consequences is called prudent. Most conduct of this kind has become so much a matter of course that we have long since ceased to think of it as having any ethical quality whatever. And it is very common for moralists to exclude all prudent activity from the field of ethics, or at the most to give it but a passing glance. Thus Kant insists repeatedly that all conduct which is induced by prudence or self-interest must be excluded from the field of ethics. He would investigate the field of disinterested or altruistic conduct alone. But the hedonist maintains not only that prudent activity is a very important branch of ethics but that in the actual systems of the past, prudence has been the vital element. Thus every moral maxim which appeals to one's judgment of value must be classed as hedonistic. When Jesus said: "Come unto me, all ye that labor and are heavy laden, and I will give you rest", he was appealing to the sentient nature of mankind. So when he said, "He that believeth on me shall be saved; and he that believeth not shall be damned". So, when he said, "In my father's house are many mansions". So the whole sermon on the mount, his most complete discourse, is entirely hedonistic." For even after command-

---

"See Matth. V; 3: VII; 27.

ing the most complete systems of non-resistance and
altruism which has ever been known[33] he adds in verse 45,
"That ye may be the children of your Father which is in
heaven". The sermon opens with the blessings which are
to fall on those who accept and follow the doctrines of the
sermon. And then it closes[34] with the remarkable parable
of the wise man who built his house upon a rock and the
foolish man who built on the sand. Wisdom and folly
are the watchwords of Hedonism. Whether we hold that
accepting the doctrines of Jesus makes a man happier or
not in this life, there is no question that Jesus meant to
to teach that his followers should have an exceeding great
reward when He came in His glory. He went about doing
good, not merely good in the abstract, not merely preach-
ing good sermons, but practical, hedonistic good. He
healed the sick, made the blind see; caused the lame to walk,
cured insanity, raised the dead, and even gladdened the
hearts of the wedding guests with excellent wine. All
through his ministry, Jesus appealed to men's sentient nature. He reasoned with them; he pointed to their misery,
discord and empty formalism, and urged them to turn to a
reasonable course of life. And whether we accept his
teaching as divine or merely human, we must admit that
he points out the value of altruistic conduct for the individual as no one else has done before or since. I do not
mean to say that there were no other important elements
in the teaching of Jesus. That teaching was religious as
well as ethical. We must also admit that an element of
asceticism is to be found in the doctrines of Jesus as they
come down to us.

More tender than stoicism and more vigorous than
epicureanism, the ethical doctrines of Jesus have done a
great deal toward the spreading of Christianity throughout the world.

The whole Jewish system of ethics is hedonistic. Even
where its demands are given as the dictates of God, they are
coupled more or less directly with the threats and prom-

---

[33]V. 33—44.
[34]VII; 24—27.

ises of Jahveh. It is true that the philosophic element was not prominent in the Jewish code. The rites and ceremonies are to be observed and performed because God has so commanded. The reward was to be directly bestowed by him, not as the natural consequence of obedience, but as a token of merit. But the formal code of conduct was too firmly instated by priest, levite and people to be shaken by the thundering arguments of Isaiah or the plaintive discourses of Jeremiah. But after all the Law of Moses was full of wise, hedonistic principles; with some exceptions it was equitable, just and wise. The land-owner, the debtor, the widow, the orphan, the criminal, and even the stranger were wisely dealt with. The criminal law was comparatively mild, the law of torts not too severe. The laws of marriage and divorce were among the best of ancient times and we know from history that Jewish family life was remarkably clean and high-toned.

Confucius, too, adopted a hedonistic theory of ethics. His theory was more philosophical than that of the early Jews. He gave more reasons for the conduct which he prescribed; that is, he pointed out the value of the conduct. Confucius, like Socrates, taught that morals and manners must begin with self knowledge. And while prescribing a minutely detailed code of action for the individual, which in the end became an incubus on Chinese civilization, yet his studies led him to see that altruism is only a wiser Hedonism; and while rejecting all religion he announced the same fundamental rule of conduct which Jesus prescribed, 500 years later, in the Golden Rule. Had Confucius been succeeded by thinkers as broad as himself, who could have put life into his moral system, China might have made wonderful progress in civilization. Unfortunately, no ruler would accept his system of government; his disciples devoted themselves to the letter of the law, and China became ensnared in an impenetrable wilderness of formalism.

Zarathustra, too, the moral and religious law-giver of the Persians, adopted hedonistic principles. Two great beings, the one light or good, and the other darkness, or evil, have been engaged in a struggle for supremacy from all eternity. But the good being is on the side of the welfare, or good of the individual; the evil or dark being is constantly endeavoring to injure mankind. In the end the good will triumph and those who are on his side will receive their reward. Zoroastrianism has many wise hedonistic maxims and principles, tending to promote the welfare of the individual and society.

Buddha, likewise, was a moral reformer. And like most moral reformers, he was stirred to thought and activity by the misery and wretchedness which he saw around him. After devoting many years to the study of the problem of evil, he reached the conclusion that happiness consists in Nirvana, or perfect peace. But the peace of Buddhism, while it frees one from suffering and is thus hedonistic, is almost the peace of non-existence. Nevertheless, all the doctrines of Buddha are based on the fundamental idea of escaping from sentient evil. The prescibed course of conduct is directed entirely toward the attainment of Nirvana, or escape from suffering. The fact that Buddha and Confucius were unable to point to a larger hope in the life beyond, as did Socrates and Jesus, does not militate against our argument. Their doctrine was negatively hedonistic, while the doctrines of Jesus and Socrates are both positively and negatively hedonistic.

Buddha, like Confucius and Zarathustra, studied the consequences of actions and with an endless prolixity of formal details, he mingles wise, hedonistic principles of conduct, based on the observation of human society, human greed and human frailty. Overburdened with the sense of the wretchedness which all the watchfulness of his guardians could not conceal from him, he left his princely home to study in peace and quiet the problem of evil. Like Moses and Confucius, he returned, fertile in plans for improving the welfare of his fellowmen. His theory of life was more spiritual than that of Confucius, but the problem which he was trying to solve was precisely the same: to wit, the problem of human misery and human happiness.

I spoke above of popular wisdom. This wisdom is set forth among every people in the form of proverbs and fables. These proverbs and fables embody the condensed and pithily expressed experience of the race. Prof. Legge says that for centuries the Chinaman has been largely guided in the conduct of his life by the excellent maxims of Confucius. Jewish literature, too, is rich in proverbs. The same is true of the Arabic, a near relative of the Hebrew. Among savage tribes the philosophy of life is usually embodied in familiar proverbs, which are passed from mouth to mouth and from father to son. Originating as they do and passing from country to country, these sayings are often couched in the most contradictory terms, and embody the most conflicting theories of life. But a careful study of them will show that they are drawn from a more or less rich experience, and that they are all based on hedonistic principles. Frequently they prescribe rules of conduct for the individual which are apparently injurious to him, and yet they are accepted as a part of the prudential philosophy of the tribe. For example, "Honesty is the best policy," announces the result of a large experience in dishonesty by the whole race. Its truth is often hard to realize, yet many a man has been governed by this simple maxim when conscience, the sense of duty, and the fear of God were unable to control his actions. Men who were unable to comprehend the reasonings of Isaiah and Socrates could lay up in memory the maxims of Solomon and the fables of Æsop. And there is reason to believe that the modern Englishman, German, or American is more influenced by the proverbs in which our languages are so rich, than he is by the subtle, metaphysical doctrines of Kant and Martineau, Luther and Edwards.

But all proverbial philosophy is professedly a prudential philosophy. It tells the individual what his predecessors have found most profitable in life. It gives him the benefit of their experiences; condenses into a line for him the biography of a race. Proverbial philosophy is often trustworthy, too. It comes with no ax to grind, no system to maintain, no party to support. Like the pebble on the river beach, it comes from no man knows where; and, like the pebble, it has been tossed and tried

until it is worn smooth and perfect. Hence the proverbial philosophy of any people is well worthy of study.
These gems of thought, these heirlooms of experience
which have survived the mutations of kingdoms and
peoples are more priceless than the treasures of princes.
And what is the burden of their tale? Is not their united
voice to the effect that, "Experience is the best teacher;"
that "your sin will find you out;"   that "The thief will
be caught in his own trap;" that "One lie makes two
more necessary;" that "If you cast your bread upon the
waters it will return to you after many days;" that "He
who sows the wind, will reap the whirlwind"? Chastity,
honesty, veracity, mercy, bravery, modesty, industry,
patience, friendliness, *shu*, or reciprocity, (the golden
word of Confucius), are all based on sound prudential
reason. The experience of the race has demonstrated and
in these proverbs embodied the fact that these virtues are
not empty forms, not incomprehensible principles, not the
dictates of a whimsical deity, not the froth of an evanes-
cent sentiment, but that they are the rational maxims of
a happy life, the fundamental principles of a moral sciene
base on human nature and solicitous for human welfare.

But not only have the professedly ethical theories
which have had the most widespread influence among
mankind drawn their main strength from their hedonistic
principles, teachings, threats and promises; not only have
the popular principles of conduct and theories of the
destiny of man, as embodied in proverbs, maxims and
omens, accepted Hedonism as the ultimate destiny of the
race, but the great religious systems of the race, which
have been already more or less closely associated with their
ethical principles and moral maxims, have likewise rested
on a similar basis. Fear and hope are the sentiments to
which religion has always appealed, fear of present or
future evil or suffering, hope of future peace or bliss.
Sometimes the evil to be escaped and the reward to be
obtained was expected in the present life, sometimes in
a more or less definite life in another world, sometimes, as
among the Buddhists, the Egyptians and some of the
Greeks, in a future earthly life (Karma transmigration);

and sometimes, as among the ancient Jews, in the lives of one's descendants.

Ancestor worship certainly sprang from hedonistic motives. A man believed in a more or less vague way that the spirits of the departed still retained power for good and evil. It was important, therefore, to keep in their good graces by offerings, sacrifices and ceremonial attentions. Where ancestor worship prevails, a man's good fortune and evil fortune, his health and his sickness, his rich harvests and his famines, his good luck and his accidents are attributed to the good or ill will of these ancestors. Hence ancestor worship, especially among people who show no great love for their kindred while they are on earth, is purely a prudential affair, almost a matter of business.

And among the idol worshipers it is very common to reproach the god for not performing his part of the contract. Sometimes he is even beaten, or mistreated in other ways to awaken him to the fact that where he has received the stipulated offerings and sacrifices, he should send the needed blessings, rain, health, good crops, game, or whatever it may be.

Even among the most highly civilized Christians this feeling still lingers. The man who goes to church regularly, is kind to his family, gives to the poor, treats his neighbor squarely, is apt to think that the Lord should prosper him and to feel abused if his crops are bad, his children are sick, or especially if a serious accident or misfortune befall him.

Hero worship is even more clearly hedonistic than ancestor worship. For the affection which might lead one to perform certain rites in memory of a beloved parent does not exist toward a departed king or ruler. One may be devoted to a good ruler, but it is because that ruler has proven serviceable, has lightened the burden of taxes, driven off the public enemy, punished internal disorder, enforced law and equity among his subjects, and broadened the opportunities of the individual to lead a happy and undisturbed life. It is the belief that the wise ruler can still do something for his subjects that leads them to curry favor with his departed spirit. It is fear of the despotic ruler that leads to the effort to appease the wrath of his departed spirit.

I have already spoken of Confucianism, the ethical religion of the Chinese, of Buddhism, the religion accepted by so many millions in India and China, and of the system of Zoroastrianism, the religion of Persia. All of these were seen to rest on hedonistic doctrines and principles. Judaism, too, was a hedonistic religion. The Old Testament is full of threats and promises. And the most frequent argument of the religious leaders was to point to the hedonistic results of obedience and disobedience. The Jew firmly believed that the conquests and other national disasters were the direct result of unfaithfulness to the Mosaic law, and that the restoration and preservation of the remnant was due to their repentance and reformation. Although they believed themselves to be God's favorite and peculiar people, they did not expect him to favor them unless they faithfully obeyed his commands; and conversely, if they were obedient, they expected the favor of heaven.

The Mohammedans are, if possible, even more hedonistic and practical in their religious beliefs and observances than the ancient Jews. Their God is a just God; and by a just God, they mean a God who stands strictly by his contract. Worship him according to his commands and he will bless you in this world and the next. Disobey him and he will punish you in this life and damn you eternally in the next. God has revealed his will, his promises and his punishments in the Koran. Follow the Koran, and your welfare for time and eternity is assured.

I have already spoken of the ethical system of Jesus. Christianity, which sprang from his teachings is commonly supposed to be opposed to all hedonistic systems. It is supposed to be a religion of self-denial, of unselfishness, of altruistic conduct. But Christianity is the child of Judaism, and, as I showed above, Jesus based all his arguments on hedonistic principles. The selfishness which Jesus and his followers condemn is the narrow selfishness which in the end is not truly self-beneficial.

Christianity claims to save men not only from the eternal penalties of their sins, but it as distinctly offers eternal happiness to those who accept the simple plan of salvation, and peace that passeth understanding throughout the earthly life. The self-denial which the Christian advocates can be accepted by the consistent hedonist,—at any rate when coupled with the blessings held out by Christianity. 'If those blessings are guaranteed, the most ardent hedonist will admit that the self-denial is worth while. It is true that the more spiritual Christians profess to base their doctrines on love and not on the hope of reward. But if heaven and hell were cancelled from the doctrines of Christianity, there is reason to fear that there would be a great falling off in the number of Christians. A few high spirits may find Kant's doctrine of duty and the doctrine of love sufficient sanctions of conduct. But for the great majority of mankind duty in the abstract and love in the abstract would prove almost totally worthless as sanctions of conduct. Common men must have a sanction of a more practical kind. The consequences of conduct must be kept before their eyes.

Even the force of habit, even the strongest religious beliefs, will not hold men to conduct which they plainly see it is to their interest to avoid. And if the promise of inconceivably rich rewards and the threats of inconceivably awful punishments have not been able to constrain men to obey the rules of Christianity with even plausible strictness, how much more would these rules be neglected if these terrible sanctions were abolished?

One feels safe in saying that even if the negative sanctions, the punishments, were abolished, the neglect of Christianity would increase in a marked degree. This, too, not only in spite of a future reward but in the face of the fact that Christianity is largely based on philosophical hedonistic principles. The reaction would be due to the fact that too many people accept Christianity through fear. They are afraid to disobey. They have not grasped the philosophy of conduct. They do not perceive that Christianity is pointing out the line of conduct which is best for the individual. They feel that they must be "good" in order to escape hell and consequently "good-ness" is always a burden to them. Because it is forced on them they dislike it, just as a school boy dislikes his studies. The same state of facts doubtless exists among the followers of all religions. Fear and not reason holds them to the mark. Here and there a thoughtful individual catches a glimpse of the beauty of holiness, of the reasonableness of the philosophy of the prescribed conduct, (if it happens to be reasonable or philosophical, which too often is not the case.) But the masses obey blindly and doggedly, because they think they must.

But if the ethical and religious thinkers who have had the greatest influence on the lives and conduct of their fellowmen have attained this result by an appeal to the sentience of their hearers, and by a demonstration of the personal advantage of accepting their doctrines, the political and economic thinkers have still more plainly and emphatically appealed to prudential reasons. Even those statesmen who have insisted most strongly on the divine origin of kings and other institutions, have felt compelled to bolster up their claims by sanctions of a sentient nature, that is, by a system of rewards and punishments. But the true statesman, the wise ruler, in all ages and nations has had the welfare of the people at heart and has sought to provide the political and economic institutions which would best promote the general welfare. Whatever additional prerogatives have been claimed for the state, the protection of the citizen from external enemies, the suppression of crime, the maintenance of good order and justice have always been recognized as falling within the sphere of duties or rights of the ruler. Moses and Manu, Solon and Lycurgus, Murua and Justinian, Washington and Gladstone all had the welfare of the people at heart. It is true that the glory of the state has sometimes blinded men's eyes to the needs of the people. But however this may have been, it is now universally admitted that the ruler should constantly have in mind the welfare of the people.

Utility, not consistency with any abstract theory, is the modern test of political and economic science. And

in the political systems of the past, it was the useful
institutions which preserved the systems and made them
acceptable. Take the Common and Statue Law of
England. It was not its theory of the divine rights of
kings, its subjection of women, its descent by primogeni-
ture, its aristocratic electoral system, or its state-
supported church which made it so strong and so
valuable. Its admirable system of justice, its Magna
Charta and Habeas Corpus, its Court of Equity and House
of Commons, and above all its constant appeal to
sentient facts and common sense were its real strength
and grandeur.

The same is true of the Roman law, from which
English law drew far more than its admirers like to
admit. The exceeding flexibility of both these systems,
where flexibility permitted improvement in the interests
of the general welfare, and their stern inflexibility where
there would have been danger to the public or the
individual good, is the secret of their inestimable value.
Unconsciously resting on the sound good sense of practical men, Roman and English law are living monuments of
the value of hedonism.

But the case for Hedonism grows clearer and stronger
as we proceed. If the political and economic systems of
the world which have proved the most durable and excellent are more obviously hedonistic than the religious and
ethical systems, the social systems of the progressive
nations show still more clearly the marks of hedonism.
This subject is so vast that one can do little more than
call attention to its more salient features.

Questions of family life, of education, of pauperism, of
the helpless and disabled, of marriage and divorce, of the
prevention and suppression of vice, of amusements, of
health and disease, trade, commerce and science, must be
determined by hedonistic rules.

The first requisite of the continued existence of the
individual and of the race is the observance of the rules of
health. No one will claim that these rules can be determined otherwise than by experience, that is, by the canon
of consequences. The final purpose of man's earthly

sojourn is not yet positively known, unless we accept the
evidence of revealed religion. Unless, therefore, conduct
which conduces to the pleasantest possible life is clearly
forbidden by an authoritative revelation, the hedonist
insists that that conduct is legitimate. More than this,
a revelation which ran counter to the laws of health would
have to be very clear and positive or intelligent men would
refuse to accept it. Such practices as self mutilation,
self torture, excessive fasting, celibacy, asceticism, and
deliberate poverty have gradually become discounte-
nanced by intelligent man. They belong to a philosophy
of pain, which, however strong a hold it may once have
held on the religious consciousness of mankind, has gradually fallen into disfavor. The number of men who
believe that God takes delight in the sufferings of any of
his creatures is rapidly decreasing and the sooner they
have all disappeared the better it will be for the race.
The religion which attempts to retard the wheels of
progress will certainly and deservedly be crushed in the
attempt. But progress means increase in intelligence,
strength, health, skill and happiness; increase in the
knowledge of the laws of nature and of the human constitution; and increase in skill in the application of the
knowledge for the benefit of humanity. Progress means
an elevation of the ideal of human destiny and an increase
in the effort to attain that ideal. Progress means the
discovery of the causes of human misery and wretchedness, and the removal of those evils, in so far as it lies
within human power to remove them. Progress means
faithfulness to truth and honesty about facts, though all
our preconceived notions and theories must be sacrificed.

IV. THE DIFFICULTIES OF HEDONISM.

A Plea for Hedonism which should neglect to examine
the many objections which have been made to the doctrine
would be a very one sided argument. The attempt to
answer all the objections which have been put forward in
opposition to our theory would be to write a book as
large as those of Thomas Aquinas and Richard Cumber-
land. But a glance at some of the chief objections will

serve to strengthen the position of Hedonism as the real guide to conduct.

1. The "Sum of Pleasures."

Among the objections most frequently advanced against our theory is that which the late Professor T. H. Green dwelt most upon, to wit: that there can be no "sum of pleasures" and that therefore it is not possible to strive for "the greatest possible sum of pleasures".

That pleasure cannot be gathered like black-berries and heaped up in baskets, everyone will admit. But that one may enjoy a greater amount of pleasure or happiness than another, everyone knows to be the case. In matters of food, two loaves are better than one; in matters of clothing, two blankets are better than one; in matters of senses, two eyes are better than one; two ears better than one; in matters of activity, two hands and two feet are better than one hand and one foot. In matters of education, two years of schooling are better than one, two hundred volumes more serviceable than one hundred; in matters of agriculture, two horses are better than one, two cows better than one, a two story house better than a one story house. So in matters of pure enjoyment, a two days vacation is preferable to one day, two chickens go farther at a picnic than one, two pounds of candy than one, two bottles of wine than one. If those who argue that there can be no summation of pleasures mean to say that there is no such thing as varying the amount of one's pleasures, they are talking against facts. If they mean anything else they do not interest either the Hedonist or the practical man.[35]

2. The Problem of Responsibility.

It is sometimes objected to the doctrine of Hedonism that it destroys human responsibility. For if each individual is his own judge as to what will promote his greatest happiness, other men have no ground for interference, even if he is mistaken. The contented swine knows his own mind better than any one else can know it, and if

---

[35]See Taylor, Prob. of Conduct, p. 330.

the wallow furnishes him the means of the purest enjoyment, creatures who do not care for the mire should not
interfere.

There is an element of truth in this contention. We
must not try to force upon a nature interests which are
wholly alien to it. By no possible contrivance can the
pig be made to enjoy the parlor as much as he enjoys his
wallow. And if it were necessary to take pig natures into
account in the state and in society, it would be necessary
to make allowance for this fact.[36] But while human tem-
peraments vary greatly, they do not vary so greatly as
do the temperament of a man and a pig. There are certain general traits which are found in all men's natures,
certain likes and dislikes, certain sympathies and antip-
athies. It is on the basis of these traits that society and
the state are constructed.[37] Within certain limits we
encourage individuality, but certain bounds must not be
passed by the individual. He must not commit murder,
arson, theft, slander, assault and battery, adultery or
nuisance. Every intelligent man is presumed to know
the evil consequences of such acts, in terms of welfare
(pleasure and pain), upon his neighbors. Their effects are
so uniformly evil that the state itself attends to their
punishment. There is an implied agreement among all
moral citizens not to commit such deeds. Other acts,
such as drunkenness, lying and rudeness the state does
not attempt to punish unless accompanied by acts of
interference with the rights of others. The child and the
lunatic are excused from responsibility for the same
reason that the dumb beast is excused. They lack the
intelligence necessary to link cause and effect. The problem at which criminologists are now working is whether
the criminal has that degree of intelligence which should
enable him to see the results of his act as they are seen by
the normal man.[38] But even if a man is lacking in intelli-

---

[36]Höffding, Ethik., p. 109.
[37]See W. Wallace, Lectures and Essays, pp. 250 and 261 et seq.
[38]Wharton, Crim. Law, I. ch. 2; Webb's Pollock on the Law of
Torts, ch. 2, p. 23. See W. Wallace, op. cit. 310.

gence, the sanctions of law and morals are sometimes binding upon him. If he knows that an act is forbidden under a given penalty, he should be punished, even if he is not able to reason out the full consequence of his act.[39] For only thus can society maintain its existence. Lunatics and small children are greatly restrained by the certainty of punishment, although they are unable to appreciate the reason for the establishment of punishment. In fact, the philosophers themselves have not yet come to an agreement as to the basis and grounds of punishment.

The limits, also, within which society shall restrain the actions of the individual are still a matter of dispute. The Socialist would have the state take charge of almost the whole human life, while the individualist would limit state control to the enforcement of the criminal law. This is not the place to follow up the discussion; suffice it to say that in our opinion the question is purely one of utility. If the majority of the citizens within a given area prefer socialism, it seems to me that they are justified in adopting such a mode of government. The individual who dislikes such a course can move away or exert his influence to reform the law. What I have said above does not amount to saying that might makes right. At least, if by right is meant the greatest welfare of the individuals of the society. For the action of the majority may really prove injurious or even destructive to the society. Such a course makes only a relative right or political right.[40] Conformity to the social law, whatever it may be, entitles one to the social approval and the escape from the sanctions of the social law. But such conformity does not ensure the actor his greatest happiness or welfare. Nor has any society more than a relative justification in adopting a law which is not for the welfare of the society. An independent people is responsible to no other earthly

---

[39]Sidgwick, Meth. of Eth., Bk. I, ch. 5; Maudsley, Responsibility in Mental Disease.

[40]Herein lies the fallacy of Hobbes, who made the political sanction to conduct absolute   Leviathan, ch. 26.

power for its acts, but that does not make its acts absolutely right.   Only correspondence with the greatest welfare of the society can make a law absolutely right.[41]   As
A. E. Taylor says, "When the evolution of ethical sentiment is complete, I am responsible to myself for obedience
to a law which I impose on myself, for the discharge of
duties which I expect of myself, and should continue to
expect, though God and man were to agree to connive at
my disregard of them[42]. In other words, when I have
adopted my ethical ideal, no matter what it may be, I
have become a law unto myself, the judge of my own
action."[43]

3. The Variability of Human Nature.

Another objection which has been often urged against
Hedonism is that human nature is so variable as to make
any standard of action based thereon of little if any value.
This objection is not substantially different from the last
preceding. What pleases my taste may be disgusting to
my neighbor. What he likes may be repulsive to me.
The tastes of youth vary from the taste of old age. The
young love activity, noise, strife, opposition. The old
love quiet, peace, unanimity, concordance. One man
loves self-assertion, boldness, courage, coolness, nerve
and skill. Another prefers humility, meekness, kindness,
affection and grace. One man prefers wealth and pomp,
praise and prominence. Another prefers a quiet nook
with his pipe and his book, or independence and rags like
Huckleberry Finn. One man is self-contained and prefers
his own company to that of any one else. Another lives
in the conversation and opinions of other men. One man
never loses sight of his own interests; his every act is a
move to promote his own welfare. Another is naturally
sympathetic. He seldom thinks of his own welfare, but is

---

[41]Since the above was written I find that Prof. William Wallace
has already expressed the same idea in much better terms. See Essays
and Lectures, pp. 253-4.

[42]A. E. Taylor, The Problem of Conduct, p. 153.

[43]Kant no doubt had this evolutionary product in mind when he
declared for the famous "categorical imperative."

always studying how he can do more to make his fellow-men happier. One man spends all his substance for the good of others. Another wears himself out devising methods for getting possession of the goods of others. Differences of temperament are familiar to us all.[44] How will the hedonist reconcile all this variability?

The hedonist will not reconcile it at all. He takes men as they are. When he finds that the benevolent disposition is for the social good, he will join with nature in encouraging such men. But the greater part of the problem nature must solve. She has probably found use for courage, anger, covetousness, and pugnacity in the past, or she would have rooted them out of human nature before this.[45] "This variability of sentiment is but the concomitant of the transition from the aboriginal type of society fitted for destructive activities, to the civilized type fitted for peaceful activities." But so long as this variability exists, of course the line of conduct of differently constituted individuals could not be expected agree in all respects.

The hedonist is not bound to lay down any hard and fast rules of conduct. He insists, on the contrary, on the greatest freedom for all in the formation and pursuit of these ideals. Certain general rules all must observe; but beyond these, there is a wide field left open for the individual choice and preference.

4. The Paradox of Hedonism.

One of the most frequently mentioned objections to Hedonism is the so-called "Paradox of Hedonism". In the briefly worded phrase of Prof. Sidgwick, "To get pleasure, one must forget it." Sidgwick and others urge that pleasure cannot be the end or aim of conduct from the fact that when we fix our thoughts too closely on the pleasure which our activities are to bring us, the result is generally disappointing. The pleasure seeker is by no means the happiest of mortals. Men who fix their

---

[44] See Lotze, Microcosmus, Bk. VII., ch. 2.
[45] See Spencer, Prin. Psyc., II, §524.

minds on the attainment of other objects than their own
pleasures are usually the most contented and happy.

Those who raise this objection neglect, it seems to me,
several important psychological phenomena. The first
of these is the law of attention. The human mind is so
constituted that the field of clear consciousness is always
narrow. And owing to the fact that human ideals must
be attained by more or less elaborate means or processes,
it is generally necessary to concentrate the attention so
closely on the means and details, that the ideal or ultimate purpose of the conduct is for the time shut out from
the field of consciousness; just as the top of the hill is
shut off by the windings of the road. These facts are so
familiar that it appears stranger that a psychologist
with the penetration which Sidgwick possessed should
overlook them. But while our ideal may be forgotten
while we are devoting attention to the means, it has not
really passed into oblivion. Jacob, for instance, during
the seven years of his service for the hand of Rachel must
have found it constantly necessary to devote his whole
attention to his work. But the ultimate reward was
before him all the time. Had Rachel died, his course of
life would have been instantly changed. Young Hanni-
bal, too, as he underwent the weary exercises necessary
to train him for the hardy life of a soldier, must have
frequently forgot his oath to destroy Rome, yet that
oath spurred him on through all trials and hardships. So
the man who devotes his life to art, science or literature
must frequently lose himself in the drudgery of essential
preparation and discipline, yet he expects the attainment
of his ideal to bring a great satisfaction and pleasure.

Once more, those who insist upon the paradox of
Hedonism, as well as those who hold that pleasure is not
the only object of desire[46] forget the sources and nature of
pleasure. For our present purposes, it is only necessary
to point out that activity as such is usually agreeable.
Compulsory inactivity is the severest punishment to most
men. For this reason the pursuit of an ideal is often as

---

[46]Especially Green, Prolog. to Ethics, p. 186 et seq.

pleasant or even pleasanter than the attainment thereof. Thus all kinds of games afford amusement, the end to be accomplished being quite subordinate. Once more, the mere contemplation or the accomplishment of success is often a sufficient motive to justify much toil and trouble, regardless of the importance of the success itself.

Some men are willing to devote a lifetime of drudgery to accomplish an ideal, which other men would regard as trivial. Others again derive their enjoyment from the struggle in which they engage, from the victories and triumphs which they secure, regardless of the actual ultimate value to themselves or others of these achievements. Again, some men prefer the enjoyment of as much inactivity as possible. Such natures would prefer an eternity of Nirvana to one of "playing on a golden harp" or other activity.

Lastly, the pleasures of some men are intellectual, those of others, emotional, and those of others, sensual. The intellectual and sensual pleasures relate more closely to the self than do the emotional. Many of the emotional pleasures arise from altruistic activities. Some men are so constituted that activity for the benefit of others is always more enjoyable to them than self-beneficial activities. For a mind so constituted, no doubt it is true that the best way to get a pleasure is to forget it. And in all the cases above mentioned, it is evident that the ideal is either a purely pleasant or agreeable one or else involves sufficient pleasure or satisfaction in its attainment to make it come under the category of Hedonism. The course of life which one prefers to follow and would willingly pursue a second time is hedonistic, whether the goal of that life or only the struggle toward that goal is the ground of that satisfaction and desirability. Untrammeled preferability is the real hedonistic test. Hence those, such as Green,[47] who attempt to distinguish between "pleasure" and "self-satisfaction" are making a limitation which Hedonism refuses to recognize. Men's preferences lie at the base of their activities. Hedonism

[47]op. cit. p. 187.

seeks to reach and guide through these preferences. In some cases the preferences themselves need enlightenment. That is the business of the scienes. In other cases new preferences are needed. This is never strictly the business of ethics—assisting nature.

V. THE PROBLEM OF ALTRUISM.

1. Pseudo Altruism.

Our purpose, then, is to outline, if possible, a philosophy of conduct; that is, to show what line of conduct is most desirable or preferable, under the circumstancs of a particular environment. So much of conduct, therefore, as can be shown to be desirable to the individual as an individual, whether it is also conducive to social welfare or not, that is, whether it is socially desirable or not, need not concern us in the present section. (Kant ruled self-benefitting acts out of the province of ethics.) For, if under every possible view of the environment, present and future, the proposed line of conduct is desirable or preferable for the individual, we must assume that the individual will follow that line of conduct if possible, as soon as he becomes aware of this fact. The trouble in the past has been that the individual took too narrow a view of the environment and was unable to see that conduct which was socially desirable was also individually desirable. Thus the advantage of association in the largest possible groups under similar laws did not become apparent to men for thousands of years. But the destruction of tribes who failed to see the advantage of larger unions, and the gradual development of the more fortunate tribes and nations which combined their strength has at last developed the idea of world empires. The advantages of universal education, of faithful fulfillment of contracts, of veracity and honesty, of chastity and sobriety, of politeness, neighborliness, considerateness and respectfulness have only gradually dawned on the human mind. That a perfectly selfish and unsympathetic man may contribute largely to the social welfare in all these and many other ways is apparent. Thus a wise man might so act among a savage tribe as to gain the

credit of being exceedingly altruistic, and yet be acting all the time in his own interest. This policy is now
very commonly pursued among enterprising merchants
and traders, not only among savages, but in the midst of
the highest civilization. From what we have,
said, it is apparent that a vast amount of conduct is credited as altruistic or disinterested which
is not so in reality. It is further apparent that much
activity is called disinterested which would not be so called
if we were well enough informed to see that the actor is
really working for his own benefit, that is, that in addition to the altruistic results of his actions they have also
self-beneficial results which amply justify them. In many
cases, too, the actor looks on these self-beneficial results
as a sort of reward for the altruistic consequences of his
acts, and is thus further supported in his action by the
consciousness of a supposed merit, a merit which would
disappear could all men clearly perceive the self-beneficial
consequences of the acts. For we do not ascribe merit to
acts whose beneficial consequences to the actor are clearly
and certainly foreseen. But these concepts of equity and
justice, which lead us daily to a thousand acts without a
thought of their having any moral quality whatsoever are
the product of age—any training of the race in social
experiences. By means of the canon of consequences, we
have become so thoroughly drilled in the more common
matters of social intercourse, that it is only with an
effort that we can perceive their moral quality. Hence
the line between pseudo-altruism and prudence is gradually
being pushed back, as men perceive the prudential advantage of a given course of action—that it is clearly to the
advantage of the actor to follow it, one ceases to attrib-
ute merit to the act. As we show in the next section,
there is reason to believe, and it is the object of Hedonism
to point out to all men, that the field of prudence will in
time cover the entire field of human voluntary activities.

    2. Rational Altruism.

    There is another important group of activities which
are commonly classed as disinterested, which on closer

examination turn out to be only a subtler form of interested activities. Take the familiar case of a man who enters an army. If uninstructed, the natural impulse would be to run when danger appears. But the wise general will explain to his soldiers that a bold front often frightens the enemy away, that even where this does not happen, that by standing firmly together each individual is really much safer than if he attempts to retreat. Following such instruction the soldier learns to face the danger and stand by his comrades when they are in danger. The importance of keeping watch is appreciated by all, and therefore when the turn of any individual comes to stand sentinel, he takes the chances of being shot for the sake of preserving himself and others, and also for the sake of having others stand sentinel when their turn comes.

Take now a more intricate case. We have indicated above that the wise man learns the value in the long run of veracity, honesty, chastity, kindness, politeness and the many other social virtues. But he also finds that these virtues can only be acquired by constant exercise. This constant exercise forms a habit. Now, when a case comes where a lie would possibly be advantageous, the habit of veracity has become so strong that the truth comes out, even while the speaker realises that it may cost his fortune or his life. A thoughtful man may have reflected on the possibility of such an occurrence early in life. But it was only a possibility and the chances in favor of its not occurring, or the net gain of truth telling may have been such as to lead him consciously to take the chances, or to take the smaller evil with the greater good. Where the whole course of conduct is profitable, then the particular instance where the course proves disadvantageous should not be classed as disinterested, especially where it was necessary to form a habit of acting in the given way in order to attain the best results. But experience teaches that all the common virtues, which on the whole are recognized by intelligent people as profitable to the actor, but which in particular instances could be departed from with advantage by the actor, can attain

their fullest usefulness only by constant and unremitted
practice all through life, thereby making them almost
mechanical by habitual practice. Thus the habit of
veracity may become so fixed as to make death easier
than falsehood. While frequent departure from the truth
makes lying so easy as to give no sting of conscience
whatever. The same is true as to faithfulness to promises.
To a man like Regulus, death by torment is preferable to
breach of promise. A man who has not trained himself
to this habitual fidelity to promises would feel amply
justified in breaking a promise extorted as was the
promise of Regulus. The same rule holds good as to pro-
fanity, to abstinence from intoxicants and sexual indulgence, and to honesty.[18] Self-culture, which is the aim of
self-discipline, is the contradictory of social justice, which
is the aim of true altruism. This self-cultivating activity
I have called rational altruism. When two habitual
virtues come into conflict, we have a curious altruistic
puzzle, such as the problem of veracity when in conflict
with the habit or impulse of kindness. Shall I lie to
prevent the wrongful death or injury of a friend? This
question has puzzled philosophers from the days of Aristotle, to those of James Martineau. Rational altruism
would apparently solve the problem in favor of veracity;
but pure altruism, submitting to the power of the altruistic sentiment, will probably always solve it in favor of
kindness.

The foregoing remarks are intended to show the
reader how narrow the margin of conflict is between
activity which is socially beneficial and that
which is beneficial for the individual but injurious
to society. The narrower this margin can be made to
appear, the easier it will be to persuade men to live
morally. For so long as you can point out to a man
that the line of conduct which you suggest is really preferable for him, is in fact that which he would follow if he
knew his own interest, you may expect that he will listen

---

[18]Taylor brings the above distinction out very clearly in Chap. V. of
his Problem of Ethics.

to you. But if you appeal to a man's conscience, to his
sense of duty, to the social welfare, or the happiness of
posterity, you may feel sure that he will listen to you
unwillingly. No one can calculate the amount of misery
which exists because men are either following unwillingly
a course of action which they feel in duty bound to
follow, but would prefer not to follow, or are living for self,
while feeling that they ought to be doing something else.
An ethical theory, therefore, which can convince men, even
in a small degree that what they think duty is really self-
interest, and what they think self-interest is really often
injurious will confer a great boon on mankind. There is
misery and wretchedness in life at best, without any more
of it based on unnecessary grounds.

3. Pure Altruism.

But after all has been said that it is possible to say in
the way of narrowing the margin of conflict between self-
interest and altruism, we must acknowledge that there is
still a margin left. The welfare of the individual, at the
present day, does not quite correspond, so far as we can
see, with the welfare of humanity. More than this,
individuals are found who are consciously acting in the
interest of society to the detriment of their own interests.
Real self-sacrifice is a fact so familiar that we cannot
shut our eyes to it. Heroism is a word to be found in
most languages, and heroes are to found in all ages and
among all peoples. Maternal love, social sympathy and
pity are too well known to be denied. Moreover, the
efforts of Bentham, James Mill and others to reduce
altruism to terms of self-interest were not successful.[49]
No doubt they had in mind the instances we have given
above of pseudo-altruism and rational altruism. But we
must admit many cases of true self-sacrifice, conscious,
deliberate self-sacrifice. How shall we account for these
cases? That self-sacrifice is not logically justifiable on
hedonistic principles we must continue to assert. But if
it is not logically justifiable, how can it be accounted for?

---

[49]Stephen, the Eng. Util., I. p. 313 et seq; II. 321.

Leslie Stephen, Herbert Spencer and S. Alexander, three of the leading evolutionary hedonists, answer the question by pointing out that our activity is determined by the ideas and emotions present at the moment of decision. Now the present idea of a future pleasure or pain may be very different from the actual pleasure or pain, when it arrives. While the idea of the suffering which another will endure, together with our own after recollections of the same, may present a very vivid motive to perform the act. Thus our own good is the motive after all. As Spencer points out, the pains of another may be as clear to us as our own future pains. Our sympathies are strongest where we have ourselves experienced the sufferings which we now see in another. And with sufferings which we have never experienced our sympathies are correspondingly weak. The actual pain or pleasure of another is not, therefore, our motive in altruistic activity, but the ideas of those pains and pleasures which exist in our own minds.

There is no doubt considerable force in this line of reasoning. Yet A. E. Taylor, in his Problem of Conduct, denies that it has any validity; taking the ground that we have no present idea of future pleasures and pains at all. But this view is certainly erroneous. I have said above that from the standpoint of Hedonism altruistic conduct is illogical. But because it is illogical, it by no means follows that it cannot be accounted for. There are other impulses of the same kind. Superstitious feelings are also illogical, but one cannot for that reason free himself from them. The child shrieks with terror when his little brother plays bear, knowing all the while that there is no real danger. Adults will do the same at the sight of an artificial snake, or even a jack-in-the-box. Many people do not like to start on a journey on Friday, or to sit at a table with twelve others, or to break a looking-glass, or to give or receive an edged present. They laugh at their own feelings, but cannot shake them off. Some people dare not stand near a precipice because the impulse to leap over is too strong to be resisted. Some

children cannot resist the impulse to handle or crush
certain objects, knowing full well that they are observed
and will be punished. A man will often find it impossible
to resist the impulse to swear, or to tell some one what he
thinks of him, even while he knows that the penalty will
be heavy. Again, the impulse to laugh often comes on us
at the most inopportune moments. We would give our
right hand to hold it back, but on it comes. The impulse
to take revenge or to wreak spite is likewise often irresistible in the face of penalties. The impulse to play tricks
is another instance. Everyone will recall children and
even adults who could not resist the opportunity to play
a practical joke, even though regretting the consequences
at the very moment of acting. Now all these are really
cases of disinterested, although not altruistic, activity.
It is irresistible. Nature has implanted certain impulses
in us which all our reason is not strong enough to over-
come. Many of our impulses can in time be brought
under control. When we perceive their evil consequences,
we make a constant effort to rid ourselves of them. But
in the case of altruistic impulses, the advantage to
society leads men to approve the acts inspired by them,
and thus they tend rather to become confirmed, because
the approval tends to make them self-interested acts.
Besides, as I have indicated above, nature selects for survival the individuals who are strongly gifted with altruistic impulses.[50] Thus these impulses tend to become
stronger from generation to generation. But the individuals who have the most vivid imaginations and can
picture the pains and pleasures of others most readily
will be those who will have the strongest sympathies. So
nature will continue to select those individuals who find
the most pleasure in promoting the pleasures of others,
and who will do the most to lessen the pains of others.
The activities inspired by these impulses are not then,
strictly speaking, a part of voluntary conduct at all.

---

[50]Dühring, Der Wert des Lebens, cited by Höffding, Hist. Mod.
Philos., II., p. 560.

They belong to the class of activities which nature takes care of—the instincts and reflex actions.[51]

As I have already indicated, Mr. Benjamin Kidd, in his Social Evolution and his Western Civilization, has emphasized more strongly than any other writer the share which nature takes in human evolution, by means of the evolution of the ethical and religious impulses. He brings a large array of facts to show that not intellectual development but moral and religious development have been the characteristics of the races which have won in the struggle for existence. The chief reason for this is that intellectual families die out. They are anxious to have their children occupy as high a grade in society as they themselves occupy, and this desire retards marriage. Thus only five out of the five hundred noble families in England can trace back their ancestry in the male line to the fifteenth century. The same is true in France and probably in all other countries. The aristocracy is constantly dying out and being replaced by a new aristocracy.[52] Mere intellectual development, however high, is not sufficient to secure the persistence of the race. It is generally conceded, for instance, that the Greeks were the most highly developed intellectually of any people who ever lived. Yet while they are still in existence, nominally, they were long ago outstripped in the race for existence, and there is probably very little if any of the blood of the ancient Atheneans now flowing in the veins of the Grecians. The old stock has entirely disappeared. They lack those traits of character which insure posterity or racial persistence. The same thing happened among the Romans. In the days of the empire the old families disappeared and were replaced by foreigners. Spain, France and England have had a similar experience. Nature, then, is constantly selecting for race preservation those individuals who have the social sentiments, love of offspring, devotion to family life, loyalty to clan, tribe, or city, pity for the weak and *mit freude* with the strong, most strongly developed.

---

[51]See Calkins, Introd. to Psyc., p. 333, et seq.

[52]See especially Soc. Evol. Chap. IX.

The variation of social sentiment may be very slight, is in fact slight; but nature never overlooks these slight variations. They may also be what we call accidental. (And that may mean mere blind chance, or the work of an unseen artificer working out a great design.) But so long as they are hereditary they answer the purpose of nature. Neither is it necessary that they be intellectually justifiable. To sacrifice self for others may seem unreasonable, but if nature impels us to do it, we must submit just as we submit to the trouble of finding food and drink when we are hungry or thirsty.

But it will be objected that this view fails to account for the high esteem which is universally accorded to self-sacrifice. Let us see. In the first place, it is natural for the recipient to approve the beneficial act. This approval is not based on the personality of the act, that is, on the fact that it was voluntarily and consciously performed by an intelligent being. For we approve the beneficial acts of nature. When the stone we throw brings down the fruit or the game, when the seed we plant grows, and when the experiment we try succeeds, we have this feeling of approval. In the next place, experience teaches us that the man who is capable of self-sacrifice is a desirable companion. The sacrificial act is an index to the character fit for society. It indicates the presence of of a "good" man, one who will not break promises, lie, steal nor in other ways prove himself unsocial. It indicates what we call a "good-natured" man. But we approve and love good-natured animals as well as good-natured men. Animals which are affectionate, tameable, not given to treachery nor to fits of anger, which are obedient and tractable, which are playful and good-humored are taken up as companions by men and loved. And who will undertake to draw a line between the altruistic activity of a brute and that of a man? The maternal instinct is as strong, if not stronger, in the former as in the latter; the gregarious or social instinct is as strong if not stronger, for man is by no means so gregarious as the herbivorous animals and certain birds. Nor is the social instinct equally developed in all men.

Even those who live in large cities often confine their
lives largely to the family. And many men prefer the
seclusion of family life on a farm, far from the crowd.
Some even prefer solitary life. The instincts of pity and
generosity are perhaps more prominent in men than in
brutes because men can perceive the consequences of
actions more clearly. And yet the instinct of pity, or
affection for the weak is certainly highly developed in
many brutes.

Again, we must remember that altruistic individuals
often cannot realize their own merits. The true hero can
not understand the admiration of others. To the affectionate mother it seems only natural for mothers to love
and care for their offspring. Her disapproval of unsympathetic parents arises from a feeling that they are lacking in "natural" traits. There is an instinctive dislike for
defective or deformed people. (Hence we call an unsympathetic parent "unnatural.") And the sympathetic feel
that the unsympathetic are defective. But to the sympathetic mother there is no feeling of special approval of
other affectionate mothers; such conduct seems "natural."[53] The same is true in even a greater degree with the
true hero. He does not feel that he has done anything
extraordinary.[54] He has simply done what his nature
called him to do. There is no sense of effort or strain,
because there is in fact no unnatural strain. The hero is
humble, because he is not conscious of having done anything to be proud of. The proud hero (and they are
numerous enough) is one who perceives the advantage of
heroism. He knows that people admire strength, beauty,
skill, endurance, energy and success, and having one or
more of these traits he admires himself and enjoys by
anticipation the pleasures of admiration and praise. He
knows that people admire and approve self-discipline as
well as self-sacrifice, and he is willing to pay the price for
the popular admiration and approval. This admiration
and approval of power, whether in form of strength,

---

[53] Stephen, Science of Ethics, p. 263; Eng. Util., i, p. 259.
[54] Jacob A. Riis, The Making of an American, p. 423.

beauty, skill, eloquence, endurance, energy, cunning, or
of training and self-discipline, is partly hereditary and
partly institutional.[55] The advantages of power, both
for the individual and for the race, is so apparent that we
should expect it to be approved and encouraged. Training and self-discipline are especially valuable both for the
individual and for the race. And the step from self-discipline to altruistic self-sacrifice is so short that it is
taken unconsciously. In our admiration for the trained
man, we usually fail to distinguish between the two. And
even the philosopher finds it hard to draw the line.[56]

4. Abnormal Altruism.

That the altruistic impulses are of natural origin is
further shown by the fact that, like selfish impulses, they
are liable to be abnormally and hence injuriously developed.
The mother may be so affectionate as to "spoil" her child,
or break down her own health.[57] The generous man may
give away all his property, thereby injuring himself and,
what is of more importance, those who are dependent on
him for a living, especially his immediate family. The
patriot usually neglects those who are immediately dependent on him.[58] The reformer is apt to do the same. The man
who is gifted with too much pity cannot be just. Rogues
and rascals constantly impose on his good-nature. This
is why it is said that women would not make good judges
or jury-men. They could not render a fair decision or
verdict. (I do not make this assertion myself, but quote
the common opinion.) The hero is not so cautious as the
selfish man, and is more apt to lose his life. Bravery
often becomes reckless daring, if not foolhardiness. The
over-sympathetic man finds it hard to tell the truth when
the truth will hurt a friend, hard to be honest when dis-

---

[55]Comp. Ladd, Phil. of Conduct, Chap. XI, p. 231.

[56]See, for instance, Bradley, Appearance and Reality, chapter on
"Goodness."

[57]See Spencer, Ethics, I, §72.

[58]"Tel soulage le miserable, qui neglige sa famille et laisse son fils
dans l'indigence."—La Bruyere, Characteres, Ch. XII, p. 375. (Ed.
1890.)

honesty will help a neighbor at the expense of a stranger. The Japanese are said to be so polite that they will commit almost any crime rather than hurt the feelings of other people.

Thus altruism presents a problem within a problem. Traits of character which were intended to preserve the race, tend when excessive to destroy the social order, and thereby the race itself. But as all altruistic activity is illogical, how shall excessive altruism be curbed? We can not reason with the altruistic person. He is acting according to his nature. All that is left to do is to disapprove such conduct so strongly that in time this disapproval will act on his feelings. Nature herself will also tend to weed out the excessively altruistic. It is this excessive altruism which Nietzsche and his followers object to.[60] Nietzsche would apparently have us select and breed men as we select and breed horses, cattle and sheep. But assuming the possibility of doing so, we must still determine the ideal character for man; and the question then arises whether the emotional or sympathetic character is not the ideal, and if so, how it may best be secured? They argue that our sympathy interferes with race evolution, and their argument is apparently just. Too much sympathy, pity and generosity tend to make the idle and shiftless more so. But Nietzsche goes too far in his demands. Even among animals, where the struggle for existence has full play, it is not the strongest and most cunning individuals that survive, but the most sympathetic. Any attempt, therefore, to lend a hand in the struggle for existence by helping the strong to survive against the weak would probably result either in the destruction of the whole race, or the nation that tried the experiment.

5. Moral Education.

It is well known that to a certain extent we can educate or repress either the selfish or the altruistic impulses in ourselves or others. Shall we educate the

---

[60]The Twilight of the Gods.

selfish and repress the altruistic emotions or the reverse?
Here again it seems to me that we must resort to the
canon of consequences.   We have pointed out above
that the most altruistic impulses are at the same time
beneficial to self. I believe that science will show in time
that those pseudo-altruistic impulses are inextricably
united with the altruistic impulses which are beneficial to
the race but prejudicial to the individual, when considered
by themselves. If this is the case, no one will want to rid
himself of those socially beneficial impulses. Thus if my
neighbor's vine has overgrown my fruit tree, I will not tear
down the vine to preserve my fruit if by tearing it down
I shall at the same time kill my tree. So in a case where
the individual interests clearly conflict with those of
society and the individual lacks the sympathetic
impulses necessary to make him strive for the social
interest rather than his own, he must still inquire whether
he should not seek to cultivate the lacking impulses for
the sake of other impulses which will accompany them.
As we pointed out above the altruistic impulses which are
beneficial to self can only be acquired by a self-discipline
that will make them practically mechanical, and when
they have become so habitual as to be reflex, or mechanical, they will act in cases which will be injurious to self as
well as in cases which are beneficial to self. In other
words, the character which wisdom requires in order to
secure the greatest possible happiness to the individual in
his environment on earth is an organic unit of an altruistic nature. He who seeks to reach the highest possible
earthly happiness by the strictly selfish road will not
succeed. The so-called paradox of Hedonism is one of the
deepest and most wonderful laws of human nature. One
must build up an altruistic character to attain such
peace on earth as is given to men to enjoy. As Maeter-
link so beautifully points out,[60] "The true sage must
suffer. He suffers, and suffering forms a constituent part
of his wisdom. He will suffer, perhaps, more than most
men, for his nature is far more complete. And being

---

[60] Wisdom and Destiny, Sec. 39.

nearer to all mankind, as the wise must ever be, his sufferings will be the greater, for the sorrows of others are his."
And yet the true sage enjoys a peace that passeth understanding. At the end of life he can say with Paul:
"I have fought a good fight." His cup of sorrow may be
fuller, but he will drink it willingly. The path of wisdom
is so sweet and peaceful, that no one would exchange it
for all the paths of temporal pleasure. Thus the
apparent conflict between self-culture and social justice is
resolved into a higher unity, just as all the apparent
conflicts in the universe resolve themselves into higher
unities when our knowledge has widened sufficiently to
perceive the broader laws. The world is full of conflicts
and contradictions for the ignorant, but as knowledge
widens, the conflicts disappear one by one, until at last
we grasp the conception of the unity of nature.

Thus pure disinterested altruism is an ineradicable
accompaniment of self-interested altruism, and hence of
Hedonism itself. Not only so, but experience proves that
purest hedonistic results may be best attained by direct-
ing the thought to the social or unselfish aspect of
conduct than by the reverse process. Yet so long as one
clearly realizes from the start that his own greatest
happiness will follow the former course, he is a consistent
hedonist. And with that knowledge constantly before
him, he will not be apt to fall into the excesses of an
abnormal altruism. Justice to self will regulate justice to
others. The ideal of self-culture will serve as a model for
social culture.

VI. CONCLUSION.

A few words will suffice by way of conclusion. Glan-
cing back over the line of our argument it will be seen that
we tried to show first that "Man's Place in Nature" has
been determined by the general course of universal evolution and is largely independent of his own desires and
wishes. We might have gone further and shown that so
far as "Man's Place in Nature" is concerned, the problem
of conduct is only a temporal problem. The evidence
points very clearly to the recent origin of the human race

on earth; and it points almost as clearly to the rather
early termination of man's earthly existence, speaking in
terms of the infinite ages of eternity. In view of these
facts, we recognized the importance for the problem of
conduct of any light which either science, theology or revelation can throw on the problem of man's nature and
ultimate destiny.

For the philosopher, the problem of earthly existence
can never seem supremely important, unless that existence is in some way related to an after life. If the earthly
life be all, the ethical problem at times seems hardly
worth the solving. And yet while this is true, there is no
ground for despising the earthly life. Moral science is
still at least as important as any of the other sciences.
As a sentient creature, man may as well make the most
of the earthly life which science and revelation will permit.
The strength of Hedonism lies in its insistance on the
worth and dignity of the earthly life, even while we are
still in uncertainty as to the after-life. It would be idle
here to attempt to force conclusions upon the reader.
The most learned men have differed in opinion as to the
nature of the evidence in favor of an after-life. Some men
find in man's moral nature satisfactory proofs of immortality. Others find the evidence insufficient and unsatis-
factory. This much is certain, however. Some myster-
ious power, which for convenience we have called nature
in this essay, is shaping man's nature in a marvelous way,
so as to adapt him more fully for social life. The human
sentiments, and particularly the altruistic and sympathetic sentiments have always played and will always continue to play a very important part in the development
of the human race. One of the objects of this essay has
been to discover just what part the involuntary part of
man's nature and what part his intelligence plays in the
matter of conduct. Our conclusion was, that the province
of intelligence tends constantly to encroach upon the
domain of the emotions. But we also found that certain
emotions, by their very nature were safe against the en-
croachments of intelligence and that as to these emotions,
to-wit: the altruistic, there is a tendency toward their

coincidence with the dictates of intelligence. When this point is reached man's character will have become ideal. Whether such a character is destined by nature to fit man for the earthly life alone or for a larger, broader, higher sphere of activity is a question which the writer will leave to the reader's own further consideration. From the stand-point of Hedonism, the earthly life, even if we concede that in some cases it is not under the present regime, will in the course of time become valuable in itself to humanity. In the mean time, ethics must ever remain the queen of all sciences. In the scale of interest and importance, ethics must ever rank above all the other intellectual inquiries of the scholar. But in thus speaking of ethics, it must be taken to include the whole problem of human destiny.

Editorial Chair.

In 1899, the University of Wooster withdrew the offer of courses of study *in absentia* for graduate degrees. Time not to exceed four years, or until June, 1903, was allowed matriculates in the Post-Graduate Department for the completion of the courses for which they had entered; but no new names were enrolled. The unusually large class that graduated with the Doctor's degree this year was due to the fact that the many matriculates, enrolled prior to the announcement in 1899 of the withdrawal of the courses for non-resident students, were unable to complete their work earlier than 1903 and were obliged to do so this year, if they were to receive degrees. All those who graduated this year were, accordingly, members of the Post-Graduate Department for at least four years; some of them for six or seven years. Even the large class that pushed their work to a finish this year were but a small minority of the members on the roll in 1899.

The Post-Graduate Department has had a history of twenty-two years. It was founded in 1881 under the presidency of Dr. Taylor, who, after his resignation of the presidency of the University in 1883, served for several years as Dean of the Post-Graduate Department. The aim of the department was to stimulate capable graduates of colleges to pursue systematic advanced courses of study in special lines, to guide such study, to test it by thorough examinations, and to reward it by suitable degrees. To this end, definite printed courses

were offered in twelve departments, and were administered by the
heads of these departments in the University under the supervision of
the faculty and with the counsel of the faculty's post-graduate committee.   The courses were revised from time to time in order to keep
them abreast of the best fresh work in the departments of thought
that were represented.   Applicants for admission to the Post-
Graduate Department were required to present evidence of graduation
from a college of good standing, except that, in very rare instances,
scholastic attainments fully equivalent to that represented by the
Bachelor's degree were accepted.   Admission could be gained only
by vote of the faculty of the University, upon recommendation of the
faculty's post-graduate committee of three members.   This committee
examined credentials carefully, and less than half of the applicants
were admitted.   Many first-class men entered for one or two courses
in the Department and pressed their work for the degree of Ph. D. to
completion in from three to six years, while others, owing to pressure
of professional work, required more than six years.   The examinations were conducted with persistent thoroughness and were much
fuller than those ordinarily given to college classes.   Many matriculates dropped the work after one or two examinations, and only a
small minority of those who entered for the Doctor's degree ever
reached the goal.   Those who completed their courses and won the
degree are, therefore, picked men, selected after many and severe
siftings.   These bear uniform testimony to the great value of their
courses for them.   The University is justly pleased with the product
of this department of its work.   Not all who bear Wooster's degree of
Doctor of Philosophy are distinguished for ability, learning and successful achievement; but, taken all together, they are a distinguished
body of men and women, a family of successful scholars to whom any
university might point with pride.   Wooster's Doctors of Philosophy
are to be found in several college presidencies, in many professorial
chairs, in important superintendencies, in many influential pulpits,
and in other places commanded only by learning and power.   Many
of them, too, have borne testimony to the fact that it was the intellectual awakening and discipline received from their Wooster post-
graduate courses that opened to them the larger opportunities.

In closing its Post-Graduate Department for non-resident work
for the Master's and the Doctor's degrees, the University does not
renounce its conviction of the legitimacy of this method of university
extension, including the conferring of degrees as a suitable reward for
the tested and satisfactory completion of the kind and amount of work
that it required for such degrees.   Its change of policy in relation to
non-resident study for degrees is due to several reasons.

First, is the fact that during these years since our courses were
organized the great increase of facilities in many of the older univer-
sities has led to an organization of graduate work far more complete,
to a supervision and guidance of resident study that mean much more

Ingram Content Group UK Ltd.
Milton Keynes UK
UKHW021943270323
419267UK00005B/261